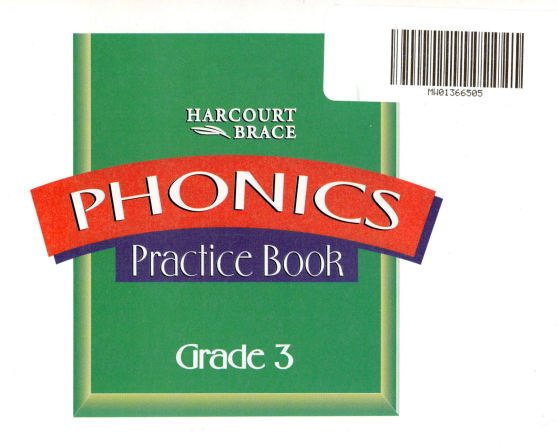

TEACHER'S EDITION

Copyright © by Harcourt Brace & Company

All rights reserved. No part of this publication may be reproduced or transmitted in any form or by any means, electronic or mechanical, including photocopy, recording, or any information storage and retrieval system, without permission in writing from the publisher.

Requests for permission to make copies of any part of the work should be mailed to: Permissions Department, Harcourt Brace & Company, 6277 Sea Harbor Drive, Orlando, Florida 32887-6777.

HARCOURT BRACE and Quill Design is a registered trademark of Harcourt Brace & Company.

Printed in the United States of America

ISBN 0-15-309035-9

10 11 12 13 14 15   073   2005 2004 2003 2002

HARCOURT BRACE & COMPANY
Orlando   Atlanta   Austin   Boston   San Francisco   Chicago   Dallas   New York
Toronto   London

CONTENTS

Unit 1: Consonants and Short Vowels 4

   Consonants 4

   Short Vowels 9

      Short *a* 9

      Short *e* 10

      Short *i* 12

      Short *o* 13

      Short *u* 15

Unit 2: Long Vowels

      Long *a* 18

      Long *e* 21

      Long *i* 24

      Long *o* 27

      Long *u* 31

Unit 3: More Work with Vowels 35

Unit 4: More Work with Consonants 48

Unit 5: Digraphs 58

Unit 6: Contractions and Possessives 63

Unit 7: Inflected Endings 65

Unit 8: Prefixes, Suffixes, and Agents 69

Cut-Out Fold-Up Books 76

Phonics Practice Book Teacher's Edition

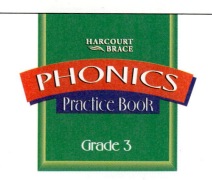

HARCOURT BRACE & COMPANY
Orlando Atlanta Austin Boston San Francisco Chicago Dallas New York
Toronto London

Copyright © by Harcourt Brace & Company

All rights reserved. No part of this publication may be reproduced or transmitted in any form or by any means, electronic or mechanical, including photocopy, recording, or any information storage and retrieval system, without permission in writing from the publisher.

Permission is hereby granted to individual teachers using the Phonics Kit or classroom quantities of the Phonics Practice Readers to photocopy complete pages from this publication in classroom quantities for instructional use and not for resale.

Duplication of this work other than by individual classroom teachers under the conditions specified above requires a license. To order a license to duplicate this work in greater than classroom quantities, contact Customer Service, Harcourt Brace & Company, 6277 Sea Harbor Drive, Orlando, FL 32887-6777. Telephone: 1-800-225-5425. Fax: 1-800-874-6418 or 407-352-3442.

HARCOURT BRACE and Quill Design is a registered trademark of Harcourt Brace & Company.

Printed in the United States of America

ISBN 0-15-309034-0

1 2 3 4 5 6 7 8 9 10   073   2000 99 98 97 96

CONTENTS

Unit 1: Consonants and Short Vowels
Initial Consonants 7
Final Consonants 13
Medial Consonants 19
Review of Initial, Medial, and Final Consonants 22
Test: Initial, Medial, and Final Consonants 24
Short Vowel: /a/*a* 26
Short Vowel: /e/*e* 31
Review of Short Vowels: /a/*a*; /e/*e* 36
Cut-Out Fold-Up Book: *Before School* (Short *a*, Short *e*) ..293
Short Vowel: /i/*i* 38
Short Vowel: /o/*o* 43
Review of Short Vowels: /i/*i*; /o/*o* 48
Short Vowel: /u/*u, ou* 50
Cut-Out Fold-Up Book: *Getting Rid of Fox* (Short *i*, Short *o*, Short *u*) ..295
Cumulative Review: Short Vowels 55
Test: Short Vowels 57
Short Vowel /e/*ea* 59

Unit 2: Long Vowels
Long Vowel: /ā/*ai, ay, a-e, ea, ei* 61
Long Vowel: /ē/*ee, ea, ie, y, ey* 73
Review of Long Vowels *a* and *e* 85
Cut-Out Fold-Up Book: *Jean's Painting* (Long *a*, Long *e*) ..297
Long Vowel: /ī/*i-e, ie, i, igh, y* 87
Long Vowel: /ō/*oa, o-e, ow, o* 99
Review of Long Vowels *i* and *o* 111
Long Vowel: /yōō/*u-e* 113
Cut-Out Fold-Up Book: *Nine Limes* (Long *i*, Long *o*, Long *u*) ..299

Phonics Practice Book 1

Cumulative Review: *Long Vowels* 119

Test: Long Vowels 121

Review of Short and Long Vowels 123

Test: Short and Long Vowels 126

Unit 3: More Work with Vowels

R-Controlled Vowel: /är/*ar* 128

R-Controlled Vowel: /ûr/*er, ur* 130

R-Controlled Vowel: /ûr/*ir* 132

R-Controlled Vowel: /ûr/*ear* 134

Review of *R*-Controlled Vowels: /är/*ar; /ûr/er, ur, ir, ear* . .136

Vowel Diphthong: /ou/*ow, ou* 138

R-Controlled Vowel: /ôr/*or, ore, our* 142

R-Controlled Vowel: /ôr/*oor, oar* 143

Review of Diphthong: /ou/*ow, ou* and *R*-Controlled
    Vowel: /ôr/*or, ore, our, oor, oar* 144

Vowel Diphthong: /oi/*oi, oy* 146

Vowel Variant: /o͞o/*oo, ou* .150

Review of /oi/*oi, oy;* /o͞o/*oo, ou* 152

Cumulative Review: /är/*ar; /ûr/er, ur, ir, ear; /ôr/or, ore,
    our, oor, oar;* /ou/*ow, ou;* /oi/*oi, oy;* /o͞o/*oo, ou* 154

R-Controlled Vowel: /ir/*ear, eer* 156

R-Controlled Vowel: /âr/*air, ear, are* 157

Review of /ir/*ear, eer; /âr/air, ear, are* 159

Cut-Out Fold-Up Book: *Carp* (*R*-Controlled Vowels) . . .301

Vowel Variant: /o͞o/*ue, ew* .161

Vowel Variant: /o͞o/*oo* 165

Vowel Variant: /o͞o/*ou, ui* 167

Review of Vowel Variant: /o͞o/*ue, ew, oo, ou, ui* 168

Schwa: /ə/*a; /əl/le; /ər/er* .170

Vowel Variant: /ô/*aw, augh, ough* 172

Review of Schwa: /ə/*a; /əl/le; /ər/er;* and
    Vowel Variant: /ô/*aw, augh, ough* 176

2   Phonics Practice Book

Cut-Out Fold-Up Book: *Bitty Bloom's Mood*
    (Vowel Diphthongs and Vowel Variants) 303

Cumulative Review: /ir/*ear, eer; /âr/air, ear, are; /o͞o/ue,
    ew, oo, ou, ui; /ə/a; /əl/le; /ər/er; /ô/aw, augh, ough* . .178

Test: R-Controlled Vowels, Vowel Diphthongs,
    Vowel Variants, and the Schwa 180

Unit 4: More Work with Consonants

Initial Clusters with *s* 182

Initial Clusters with *r* 184

Initial Clusters with *l* 186

Initial Clusters with *w* 188

Review of Initial Clusters *s, r, l, w* 190

Initial Clusters *scr-, str-, spr-, squ-* 192

Final Clusters with *t (st, nt, lt, ft)* 196

Final Clusters *lk, sk, sp, ld, mp, nd* 198

Review of Initial Clusters *scr-, str-, spr-, squ-;* Final Clusters
    with *t;* and Final Clusters *lk, sk, sp, ld, mp, nd* 200

Hard and Soft *c* 202

Hard and Soft *g* 208

Review of Hard and Soft *c* and *g* 214

Cumulative Review: Consonant Clusters, Hard and
    Soft *c* and *g* 216

Test: Consonant Clusters, Hard and Soft *c* and *g* 218

Unit 5: Digraphs

Digraph: Initial /ch/*ch* 220

Digraph: Final /ch/*ch, tch* .221

Digraph: Initial and Final /sh/*sh;* Initial Cluster: /shr/*shr* . .222

Digraph: Initial and Final /th/*th;* Initial Cluster: /thr/*thr* . .224

Digraph: Initial /hw/*wh* 226

Phonics Practice Book   3

Review of Digraphs: Initial /ch/*ch;* Final /ch/*ch, tch;*
    Initial and Final /sh/*sh;* Initial Cluster: /shr/*shr;*
    Initial and Final /th/*th;* Initial Cluster: /thr/*thr;*
    Initial /hw/*wh* 228

Digraph: Initial and Final /f/*ph* 230

Digraph: Final /f/*gh* 231

Digraph: Initial /r/*wr* 232

Digraph: Initial /n/*kn, gn* 233

Digraphs: Final /ng/*ng;* /ngk/*nk* 234

Review of Digraphs: /f/*ph, gh; /r/wr; /n/kn, gn;*
    Final /ng/*ng;* /ngk/*nk* 236

Test: Digraphs 238

Unit 6: Contractions and Possessives

Contractions: *'m, n't, 'll, 's* .240

Contractions: *'d, 've, 're* 241

Review of Contractions 242

Possessive: *'s* 244

Possessive: *s'* 245

Review of Possessives 246

Test: Contractions 248

Test: Possessives 249

Unit 7: Inflected Endings

Inflected Endings: *-s, -es, -ed, -ing* 250

Inflected Endings: *-ed, -ing* (double final consonant) 252

Review of Inflected Endings: *-s, -es, -ed, -ing* 254

Inflected Endings: *-ed, -ing* (drop final *e*) 256

Inflected Ending: *-es* (change *f* to *v*) 258

Inflected Ending: *-ies* (drop final *y*) 259

Cumulative Review: Inflected Endings 261

Test: Inflected Endings 263

4   Phonics Practice Book

Unit 8: Prefixes, Suffixes, and Agents

Prefixes: *un-, re-, im-* 265

Prefixes: *non-, pre-, dis-* 268

Review of Prefixes 271

Suffixes: *-ly, -ful* 273

Suffixes: *-able, -less* 275

Review of Suffixes 277

Cumulative Review: Prefixes and Suffixes 279

Comparatives and Superlatives (*-er, -est*) 281

Comparatives and Superlatives (*more, most*) 283

Agents: *-or, -er* 285

Review of Comparatives and Superlatives and Agents . . .287

Cumulative Review: Prefixes, Suffixes, Comparatives
    and Superlatives, and Agents 289

Test: Prefixes, Suffixes, Comparatives and Superlatives,
    and Agents 291

Cut-Out Fold-Up Books

Before School (Short *a,* Short *e*) 293

Getting Rid of Fox (Short *i,* Short *o,* Short *u*) 295

Jean's Painting (Long *a,* Long *e*) 297

Nine Limes (Long *i,* Long *o,* Long *u*) 299

Carp (*R*-Controlled Vowels) 301

Bitty Bloom's Mood (Vowel Diphthongs and
    Vowel Variants) 303

Phonics Practice Book   5

4

Phonics Practice Book Teacher's Edition

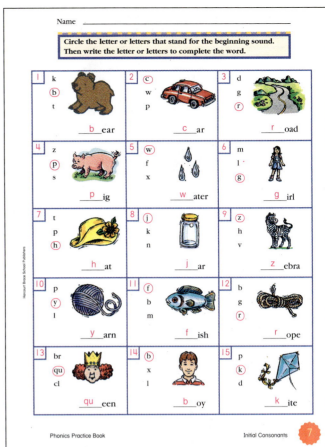

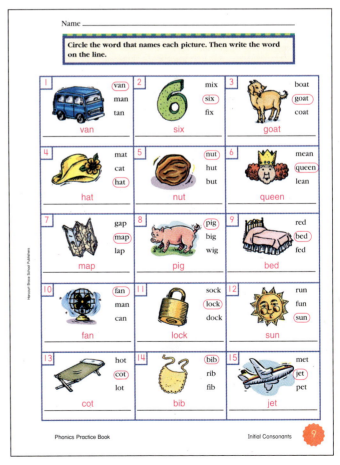

Phonics Practice Book Teacher's Edition

5

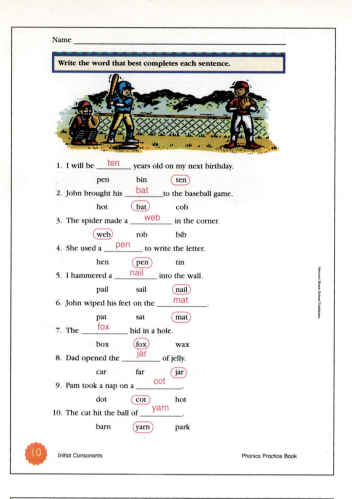
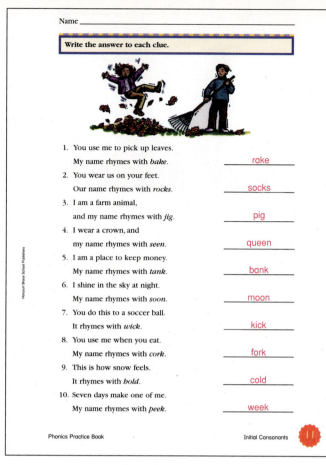
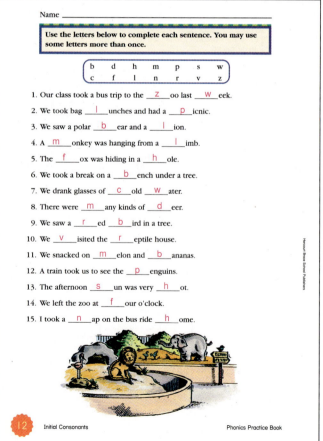

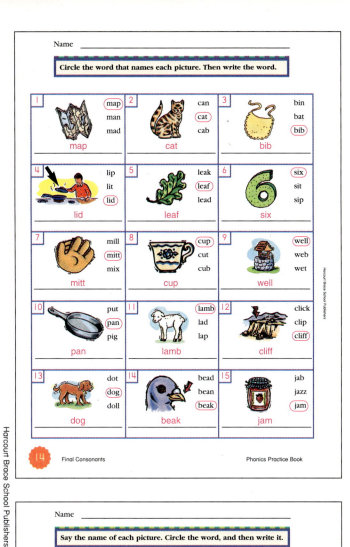
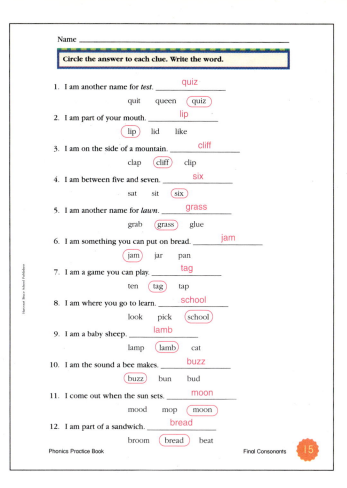
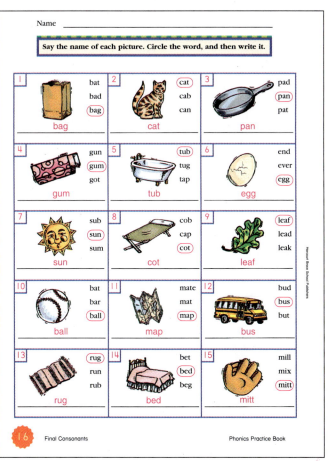
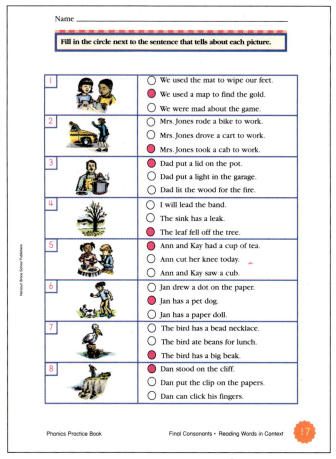

Phonics Practice Book Teacher's Edition　　7

Name _____

Use letters below to complete the sentences in the story. You may use some letters more than once.

p m k d n g t x w

The Jones family wen_t_ to a far_m_ near their tow_n_. Don and Pat helped fee_d_ the chickens, the pigs, and the co_w_. Dad saw a ma_n_ mil_k_ the co_w_. Mom gathered eggs from the he_n_.

Mom and Pat made ja_m_ in a pa_n_. Don saw a little chic_k_ in a bo_x_. Dad picked cor_n_ in the garde_n_.

For lunch, the Jones family ate corn, ha_m_, sala_d_, and warm bread with honey. They had ice crea_m_ for dessert. Then Pat and Don played ta_g_ in the yar_d_. Mom read a boo_k_ while Dad took a na_p_.

18 Final Consonants • Reading Words in Context   Phonics Practice Book

---

Name _____

Say the name of each picture. Write the letter that stands for the sound you hear in the middle of the word.

1. ti_g_er	2. ca_b_in	3. spi_d_er
4. ru_l_er	5. ca_m_el	6. pea_n_ut
7. pa_p_er	8. sa_l_ad	9. wa_g_on
10. mo_n_ey	11. mu_s_ic	12. ba_b_y
13. le_m_on	14. wa_t_er	15. me_t_er
16. co_l_or	17. de_s_ert	18. pia_n_o

Phonics Practice Book   Medial Consonants 19

Name _____

Write the word that answers each clue. You will not use all the words.

melon	desert	tulip	honey	wagon	baby
spider	paper	money	tiger	sweater	robin
camel	water	ruler	music	dragon	tuba

1. You can buy things with me.   money
2. You can draw on me.   paper
3. I am a fruit you can eat.   melon
4. I make a web.   spider
5. I taste very sweet.   honey/melon
6. You can ride in me.   wagon
7. Put me on when you are cold.   sweater
8. I help you draw a straight line.   ruler
9. You hear me on the radio.   music/tuba
10. My nest is in a tree.   robin
11. Drink me when you are thirsty.   water
12. I am a make-believe animal.   dragon
13. You can see me in a band.   tuba
14. I grow in the spring.   tulip
15. I am a hot, dry place that gets little rain. desert

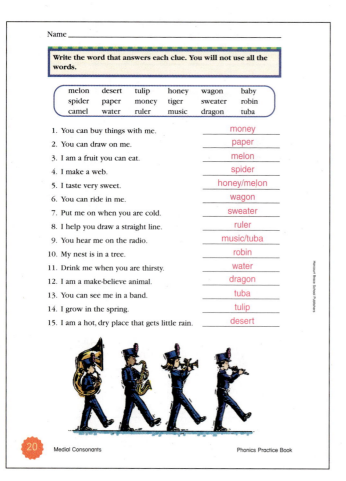

20 Medial Consonants   Phonics Practice Book

Name _____

Fill in the circle next to the sentence that tells about each picture.

1. ● Dad took Betsy to the zoo.
   ○ Dad took the dragon to the zoo.
   ○ Dad took the robin to the zoo.

2. ● Dad found a spiderweb in the corner.
   ○ Dad found a beaver in the corner.
   ○ The spiderweb was on the tiger.

3. ○ The camel swam in the river.
   ○ They saw a camel in the desert.
   ● They rode a camel around the park.

4. ○ Dad and Betsy made some money.
   ● Dad and Betsy listened to some music.
   ○ Dad and Betsy were in a band.

5. ○ Salad is good for lunch.
   ○ A woman was on the bench.
   ● They ate melon on the bench.

6. ○ Betsy poured a glass of juice.
   ○ A robin splashed in the water.
   ● Dad helped Betsy get some water.

Phonics Practice Book   Medial Consonants • Reading Words in Context 21

---

8   Phonics Practice Book Teacher's Edition

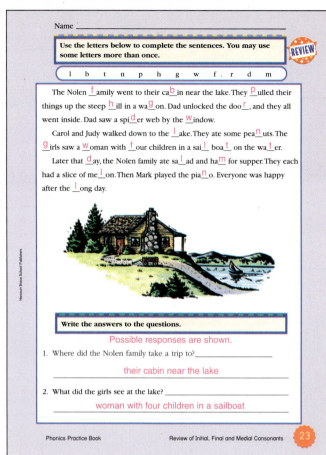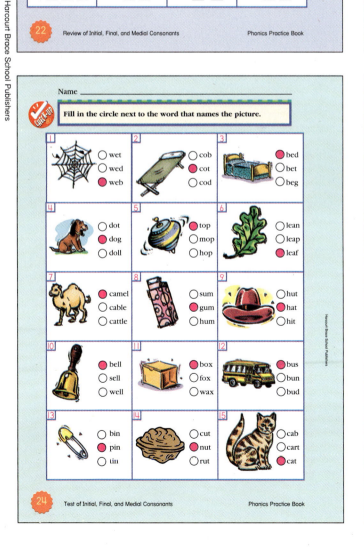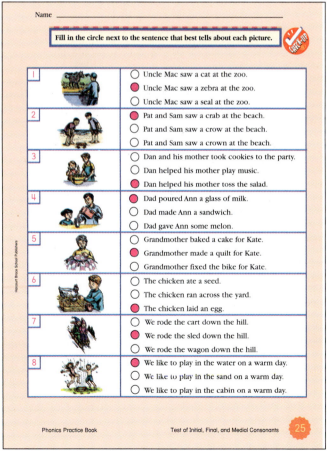

Phonics Practice Book Teacher's Edition

9

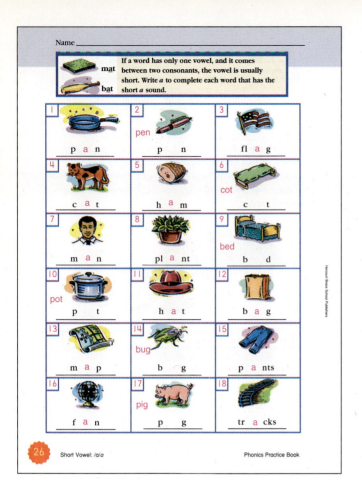
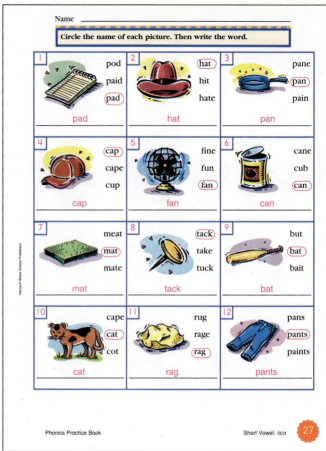
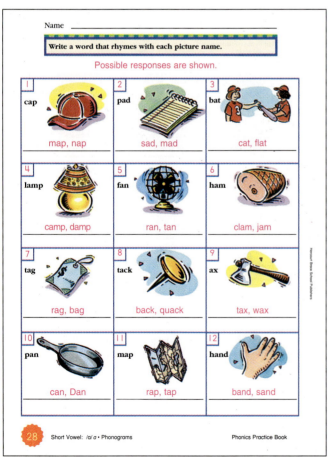
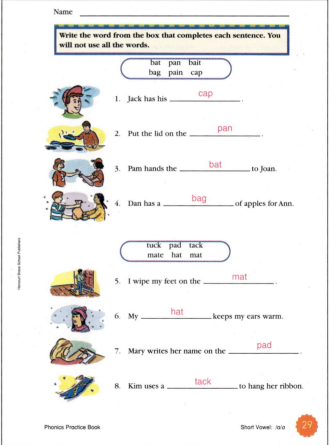

10

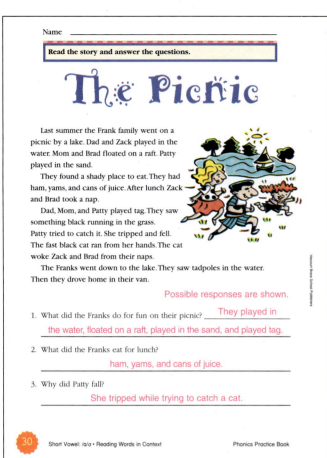
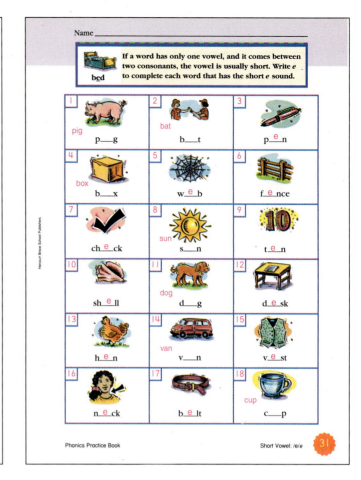
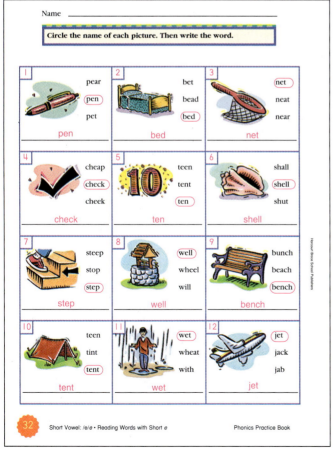
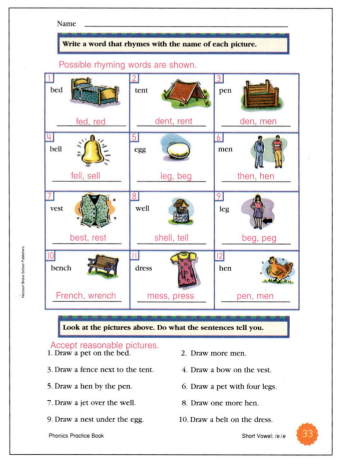

Name _____

Write the word that completes each sentence. You will not use all the words.

| Red | pen | put | pet | fed |

1. Jeff got a dog for a _____ pet _____.
2. Jeff said, "I will call you _____ Red _____."
3. Jeff _____ fed _____ his dog a snack.
4. Jeff made a _____ pen _____ for Red in the yard.

| bed | Teen | beg | Ten | led |

5. Jeff showed Red how to _____ beg _____.
6. Jeff _____ led _____ Red on a short walk.
7. Jeff made a _____ bed _____ for Red.
8. Jeff said, "_____ Ten _____ o'clock. Time for bed."

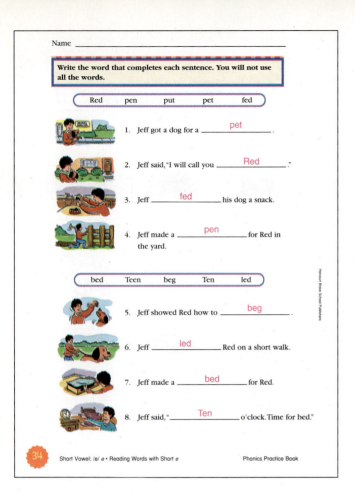

34   Short Vowel: /e/ e • Reading Words with Short e   Phonics Practice Book

---

Name _____

Read the poem. Then write the answers to the questions.

Ned and Ted's Hike

Ned went for a hike with Ted,
Up and down where the path led.
They saw a spider in a web,
And a boy whose name was Jeb.
They saw a red bird in a nest,
And a girl called Jen in a vest.
They saw a bug with six black legs,
And a hen with lots of eggs.
They saw a fox outside its den,
And some rabbits in a pen.
Then Ned and Ted went home to rest,
And tell Aunt Meg what they liked best.

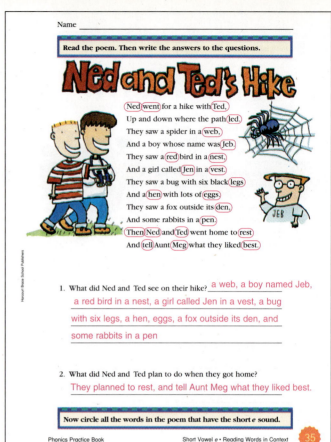

1. What did Ned and Ted see on their hike? a web, a boy named Jeb, a red bird in a nest, a girl called Jen in a vest, a bug with six legs, a hen, eggs, a fox outside its den, and some rabbits in a pen

2. What did Ned and Ted plan to do when they got home? They planned to rest, and tell Aunt Meg what they liked best.

Now circle all the words in the poem that have the short *e* sound.

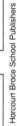

Phonics Practice Book   Short Vowel e • Reading Words in Context   35

Name _____

REVIEW — **Write the word that names the picture.**

1. map	2. bed	3. hen
4. bag	5. pen	6. van
7. men	8. ham	9. ten
10. leg	11. cat	12. bat
13. web	14. hat	15. belt

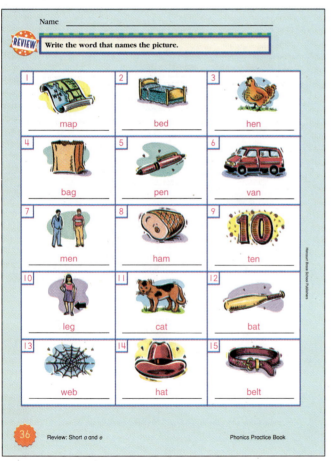

36   Review: Short a and e   Phonics Practice Book

Name _____

Write the word that answers each clue. You will not use all of the words.

| jam | ten | pan | pen | cap | cup | cab | bed | tan |

1. You can ride in it. _____ cab
2. We eat it on bread. _____ jam
3. It comes after nine. _____ ten
4. You can write with it. _____ pen
5. You wear it on your head. _____ cap
6. You can sleep in it. _____ bed

| bet | smell | stem | bat | red | stream | fast | bell | reed |

7. You hit a ball with it. _____ bat
8. You hold this part of a flower. _____ stem
9. It tells how some people run. _____ fast
10. It is a color in the American flag. _____ red
11. You hear it ring. _____ bell
12. You do this with your nose. _____ smell

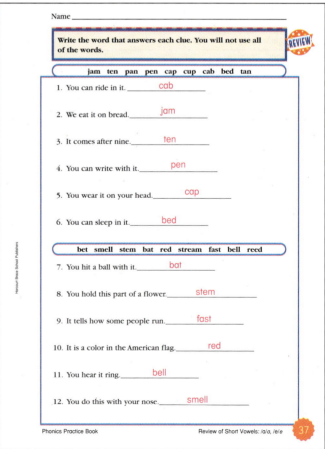

Phonics Practice Book   Review of Short Vowels: /a/a, /e/e   37

---

12   Phonics Practice Book Teacher's Edition

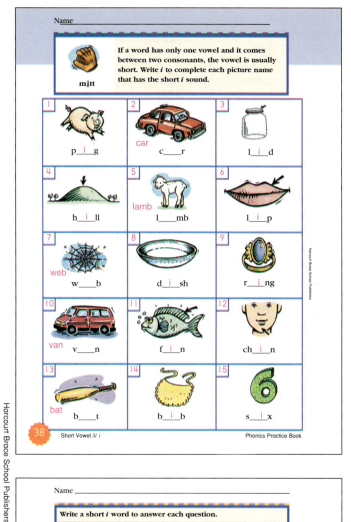
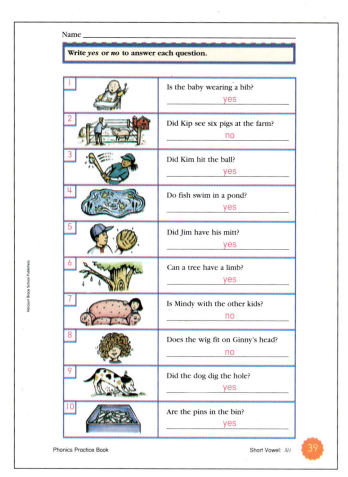
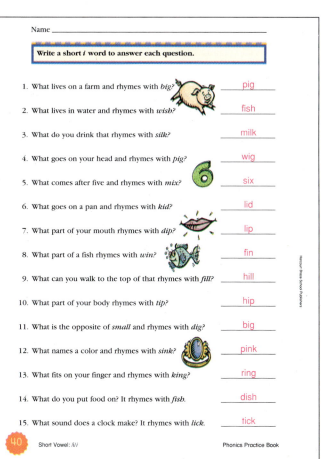
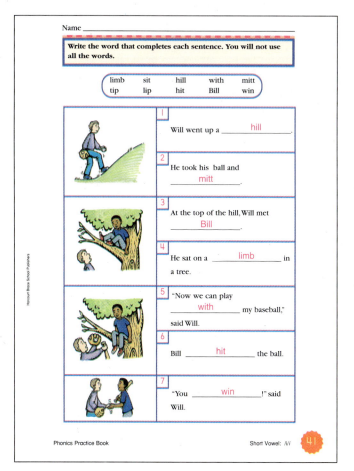

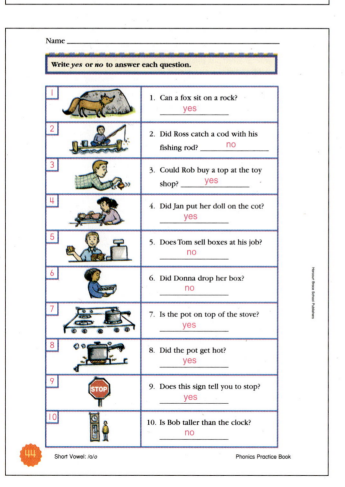
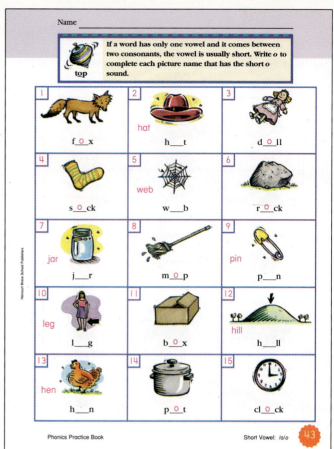
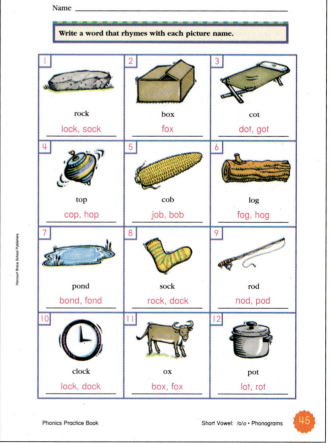

Phonics Practice Book Teacher's Edition

Name _____

Write the word that completes each sentence. You will not use all the words.

mop	cob	hot	Jon	mom
pot	lock	stop	box	got

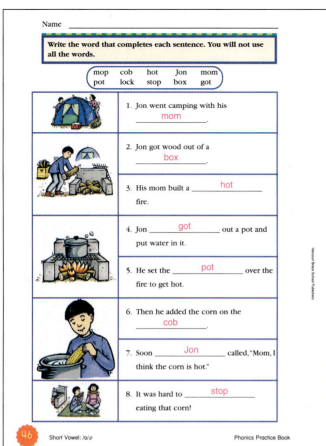

1. Jon went camping with his ____**mom**____.
2. Jon got wood out of a ____**box**____.
3. His mom built a ____**hot**____ fire.
4. Jon ____**got**____ out a pot and put water in it.
5. He set the ____**pot**____ over the fire to get hot.
6. Then he added the corn on the ____**cob**____.
7. Soon ____**Jon**____ called, "Mom, I think the corn is hot."
8. It was hard to ____**stop**____ eating that corn!

46 Short Vowel: /o/o — Phonics Practice Book

Name _____

Read the story. Then answer the questions.

The Top of the World

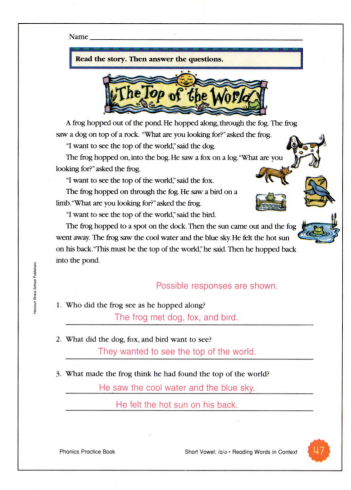

A frog hopped out of the pond. He hopped along, through the fog. The frog saw a dog on top of a rock. "What are you looking for?" asked the frog.

"I want to see the top of the world," said the dog.

The frog hopped on, into the bog. He saw a fox on a log. "What are you looking for?" asked the frog.

"I want to see the top of the world," said the fox.

The frog hopped on through the fog. He saw a bird on a limb. "What are you looking for?" asked the frog.

"I want to see the top of the world," said the bird.

The frog hopped to a spot on the dock. Then the sun came out and the fog went away. The frog saw the cool water and the blue sky. He felt the hot sun on his back. "This must be the top of the world," he said. Then he hopped back into the pond.

Possible responses are shown.

1. Who did the frog see as he hopped along?
   The frog met dog, fox, and bird.

2. What did the dog, fox, and bird want to see?
   They wanted to see the top of the world.

3. What made the frog think he had found the top of the world?
   He saw the cool water and the blue sky.
   He felt the hot sun on his back.

Phonics Practice Book — Short Vowel: /o/o • Reading Words in Context 47

Name _____

REVIEW — Circle the letter that stands for the short vowel sound in each picture name.

1. box — a, e, **o**
2. log — e, **o**, i
3. hill — **i**, o, a
4. pig — e, o, **i**
5. mop — **o**, e, i
6. mitt — a, **i**, o
7. doll — i, **o**, e
8. pins — **i**, o, e
9. wig — a, **i**, e
10. fox — **o**, e, i
11. cot — i, **o**, a
12. clock — i, a, **o**
13. bib — a, **i**, o
14. sock — a, **o**, i
15. six — **i**, o, e

48 Review of Short Vowels i and o — Phonics Practice Book

Name _____

REVIEW — Circle the answer to each clue. Then write the word on the line.

1. It is part of your mouth. ____**lip**____
   (lip) lap leap

2. You put this on your foot. ____**sock**____
   sack (sock) sick

3. You need a key to open this. ____**lock**____
   lake (lock) lick

4. This animal lives on a farm. ____**pig**____
   (pig) peg pain

5. When you go camping, you sleep on this. ____**cot**____
   (cot) cat cut

6. A baby wears this. ____**bib**____
   bob (bib) bud

7. You hold this when you go fishing. ____**rod**____
   rid red (rod)

8. You use a shovel to do this. ____**dig**____
   dog (dig) dime

9. You can climb to the top of this. ____**hill**____
   hall heel (hill)

10. This animal hops and likes the water. ____**frog**____
    (frog) flip float

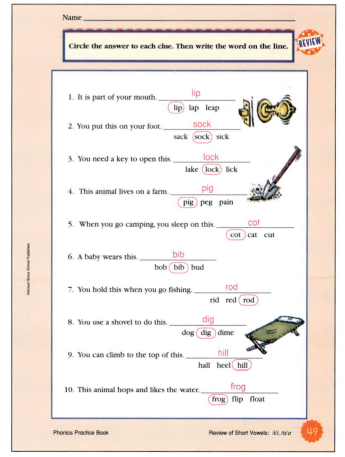

Phonics Practice Book — Review of Short Vowels: /i/i, /o/o 49

Phonics Practice Book Teacher's Edition — 15

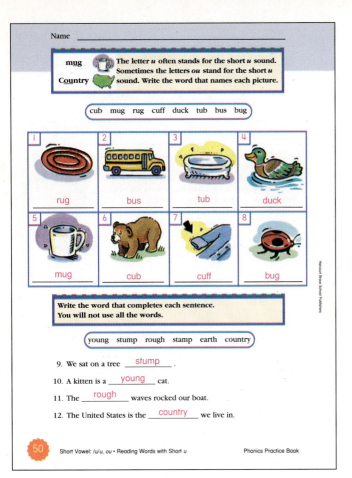

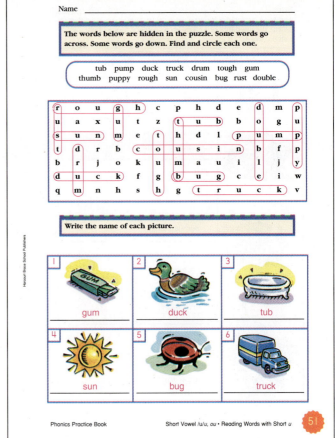

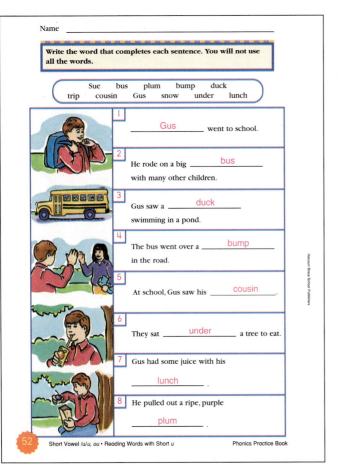

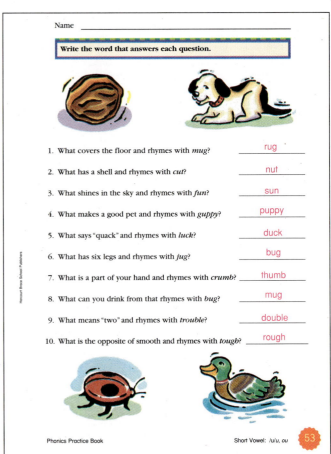

16

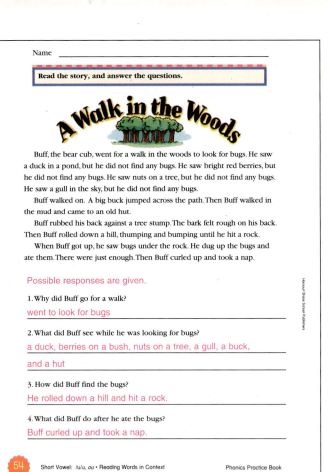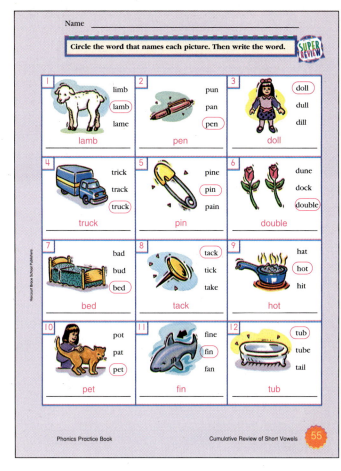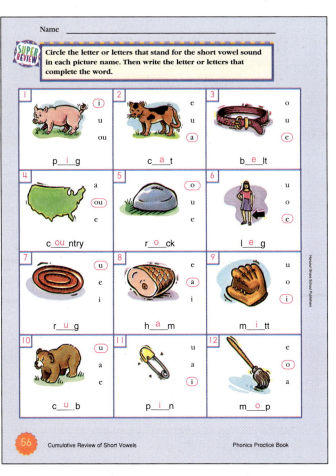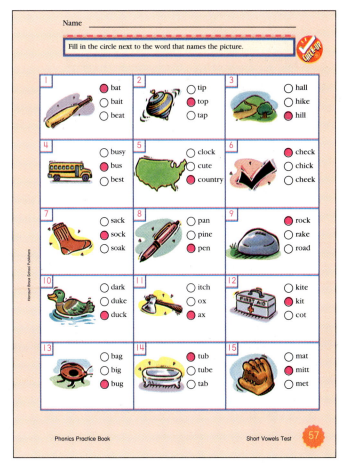

Phonics Practice Book Teacher's Edition

17

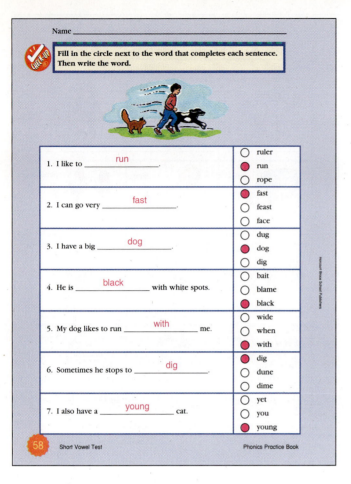
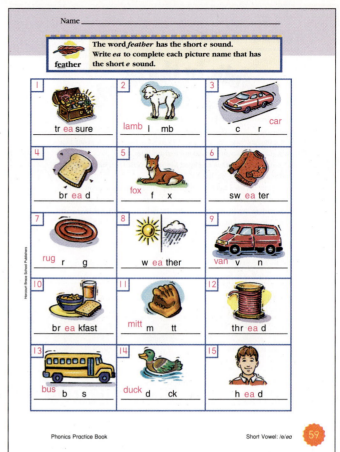
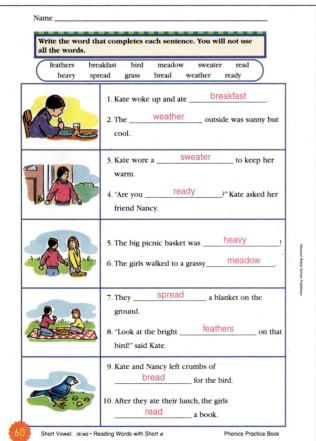
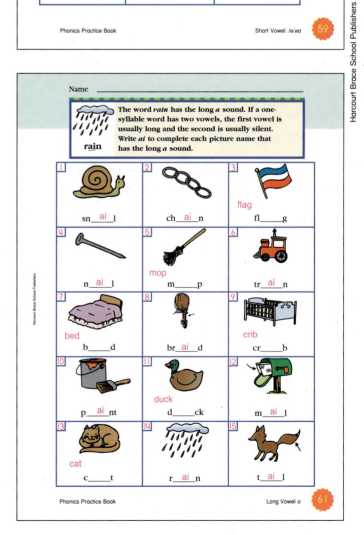

Phonics Practice Book Teacher's Edition

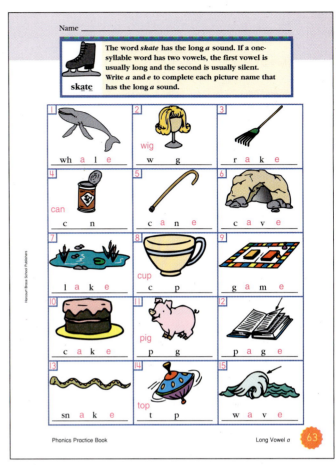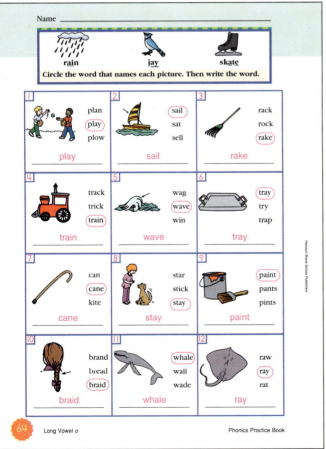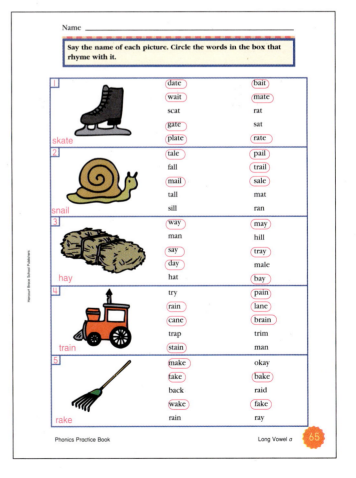

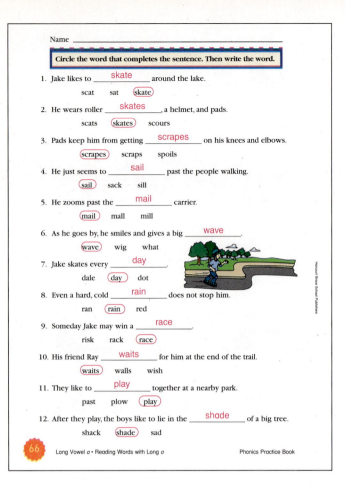

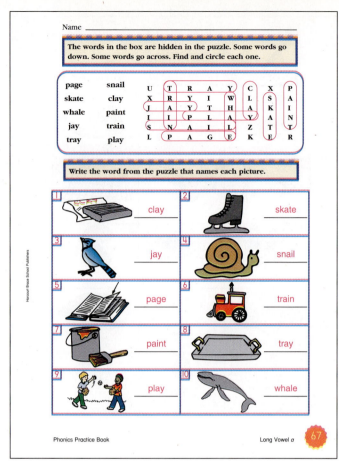

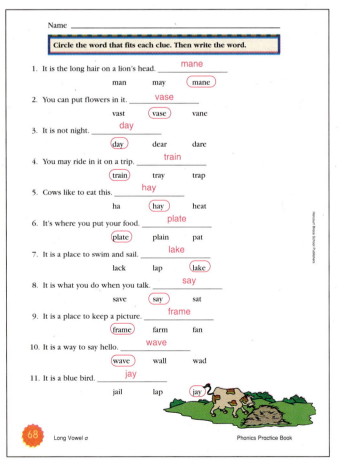

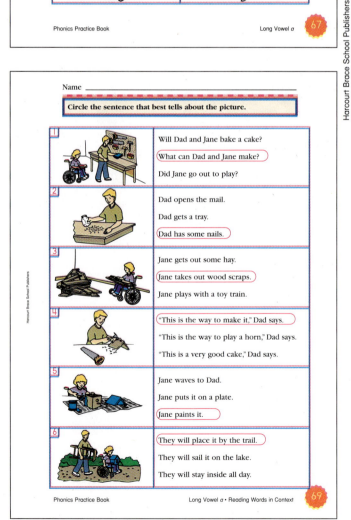

20

Phonics Practice Book Teacher's Edition

Name _____

eight **veil** The letters *ei* and *eigh* can stand for the long *a* sound. Circle the word that names the picture. Then write the word.

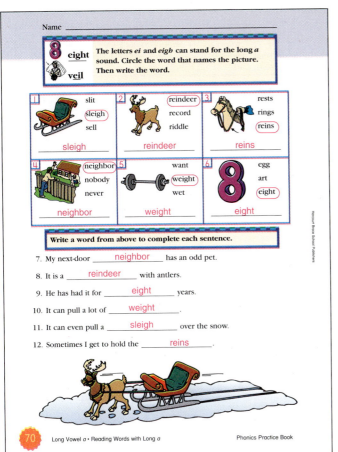

1. slit / (sleigh) / sell — sleigh
2. (reindeer) / record / riddle — reindeer
3. rests / rings / (reins) — reins
4. (neighbor) / nobody / never — neighbor
5. want / (weight) / wet — weight
6. egg / art / (eight) — eight

Write a word from above to complete each sentence.

7. My next-door __neighbor__ has an odd pet.
8. It is a __reindeer__ with antlers.
9. He has had it for __eight__ years.
10. It can pull a lot of __weight__.
11. It can even pull a __sleigh__ over the snow.
12. Sometimes I get to hold the __reins__.

70 Long Vowel *a* • Reading Words with Long *a* Phonics Practice Book

---

Name _____

break The letters *ea* can stand for the long *a* sound. Write the word that answers each clue. You will not use all of the words.

braid	May	page	snail	tray
break	great	paint	steak	wave
hay	neighbor	play	train	whale

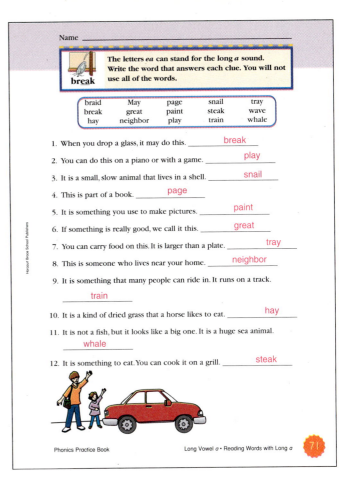

1. When you drop a glass, it may do this. __break__
2. You can do this on a piano or with a game. __play__
3. It is a small, slow animal that lives in a shell. __snail__
4. This is part of a book. __page__
5. It is something you use to make pictures. __paint__
6. If something is really good, we call it this. __great__
7. You can carry food on this. It is larger than a plate. __tray__
8. This is someone who lives near your home. __neighbor__
9. It is something that many people can ride in. It runs on a track. __train__
10. It is a kind of dried grass that a horse likes to eat. __hay__
11. It is not a fish, but it looks like a big one. It is a huge sea animal. __whale__
12. It is something to eat. You can cook it on a grill. __steak__

Long Vowel *a* • Reading Words with Long *a* 71

Name _____

Write each word under the correct heading.

baby	crayon	neighbor	plate	snake
baker	lady	weight	reindeer	stingray
clay	mayor	paint	snail	whale

People	Animals	Things
baby	reindeer	clay
baker	snail	crayon
lady	snake	weight
mayor	stingray	paint
neighbor	whale	plate

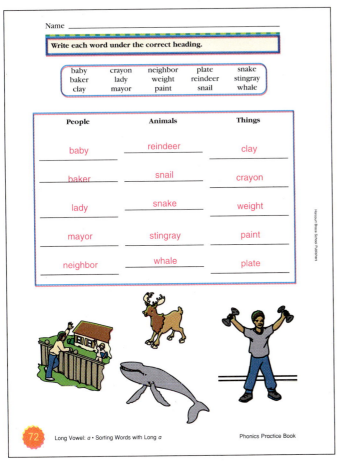

72 Long Vowel: *a* • Sorting Words with Long *a* Phonics Practice Book

---

Name _____

heel The letters *ee* in *heel* stand for the long *e* sound. If a one-syllable word has two vowels, the first vowel is usually long and the second is usually silent. Write *ee* to complete each picture name that has the long *e* sound.

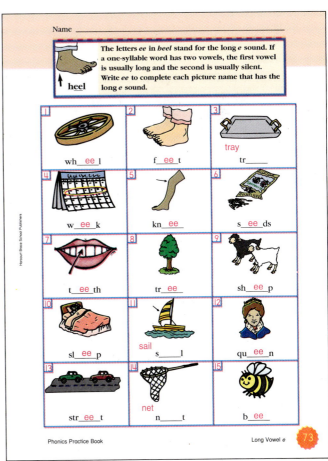

1. wh__ee__l
2. f__ee__t
3. tr____
4. w__ee__k
5. kn__ee__
6. s__ee__ds
7. t__ee__th
8. tr__ee__
9. sh__ee__p
10. sl__ee__p
11. s____l
12. qu__ee__n
13. str__ee__t
14. n____t
15. b__ee__

Phonics Practice Book Long Vowel *e* 73

Phonics Practice Book Teacher's Edition 21

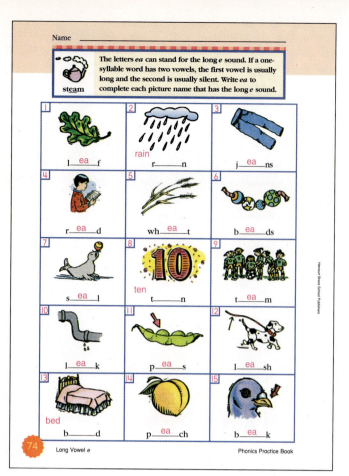
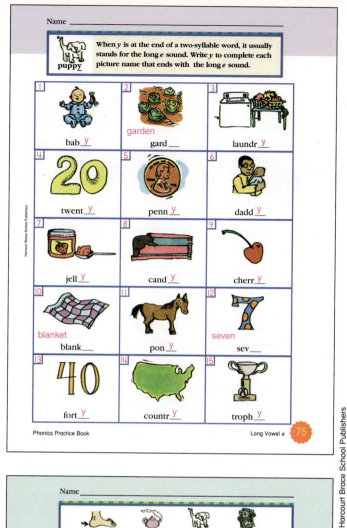
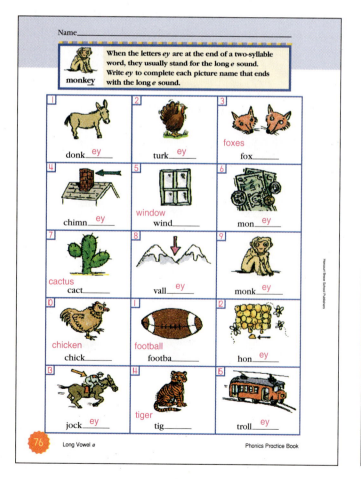
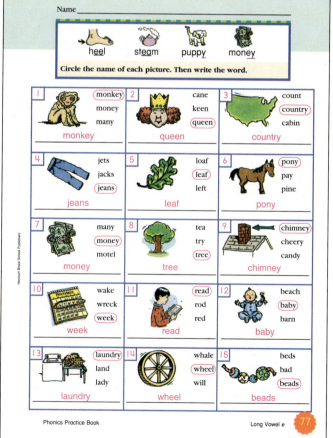

Name _____

Say the name of each picture. Circle the words that rhyme with it.

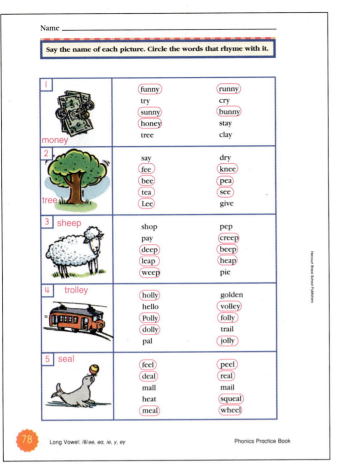

1. money	(funny) try (sunny) (honey) tree	(runny) cry (bunny) stay clay
2. tree	say (fee) (bee) (tea) (Lee)	dry (knee) (pea) (see) give
3. sheep	shop pay (deep) (leap) (weep)	pep (creep) (beep) (heap) pie
4. trolley	(holly) hello (Polly) (dolly) pal	golden (volley) (folly) trail (jolly)
5. seal	(feel) (deal) mall heat (meal)	(peel) (real) mail (squeal) (wheel)

78 — Long Vowel: /ē/ ee, ea, ie, y, ey

Name _____

Circle the word that best completes the sentence. Then write the word.

1. If you get a __puppy__, you must train it and care for it.
   (puppy) pipe padlock
2. You have to __feed__ it every day.
   (feed) foot fever
3. You also have to give it water __each__ day.
   ache (each) enter
4. You need to brush the puppy and protect it from __fleas__.
   flaps (fleas) flutes
5. You __need__ to be kind and loving to the puppy.
   next not (need)
6. Training a puppy is never __easy__.
   eating (easy) eggs
7. You should __speak__ to it in a soft voice.
   (speak) spark speck
8. You should take it for a walk after each __meal__.
   men mail (meal)
9. The puppy will have to get used to wearing its __leash__.
   lash leak (leash)

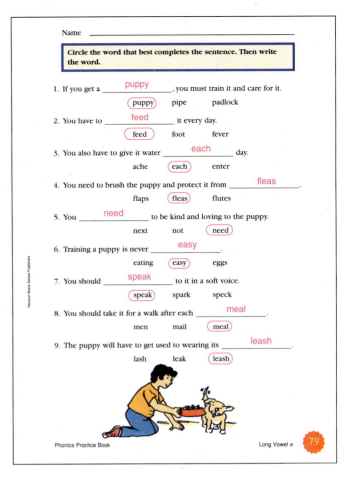

79 — Long Vowel e

Name _____

Choose the word that fits each clue. Write the words in the puzzle.

cheek	knee	street
chimney	party	tea
eat	please	teeth
happy	read	turkey
	sea	

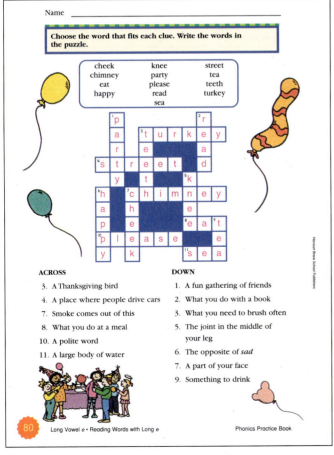

Crossword:
1. p a r t y
2. r e a d
3. t u r k e y
4. s t r e e t
5. k
6. h
7. c h i m n e y
8. e a t
9. e
10. p l e a s e
11. s e a

ACROSS
3. A Thanksgiving bird
4. A place where people drive cars
7. Smoke comes out of this
8. What you do at a meal
10. A polite word
11. A large body of water

DOWN
1. A fun gathering of friends
2. What you do with a book
3. What you need to brush often
5. The joint in the middle of your leg
6. The opposite of *sad*
7. A part of your face
9. Something to drink

80 — Long Vowel e • Reading Words with Long e

Name _____

Circle the word that fits each clue. Then write the word.

1. This is what we do with food. __eat__
   yet end (eat)
2. This fruit makes a juicy snack. __peach__
   pest (peach) please
3. The bread we eat is made from this grain. __wheat__
   whale (wheat) wet
4. This small red fruit grows on trees. __cherry__
   (cherry) cheer check
5. Many people grill or bake this food. __meat__
   met (meat) marry
6. Some people eat this with stuffing and gravy. __turkey__
   turtle tunnel (turkey)
7. Desserts taste this way. __sweet__
   (sweet) set sleep
8. This is a treat you should not eat too often. __candy__
   city (candy) chimney
9. You should floss these each day. __teeth__
   teach tell (teeth)
10. It is fun to eat meals with them. __family__
    feel (family) free

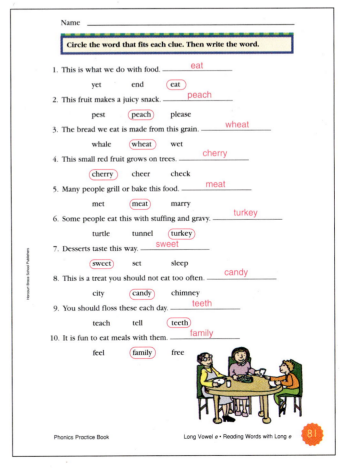

81 — Long Vowel e • Reading Words with Long e

Phonics Practice Book Teacher's Edition   23

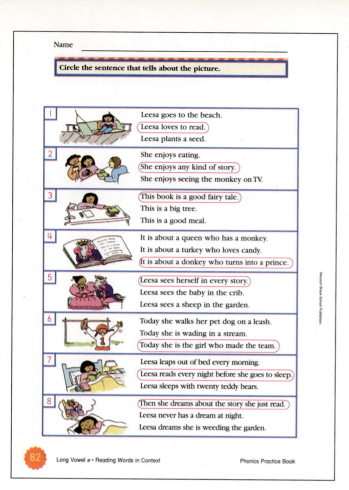
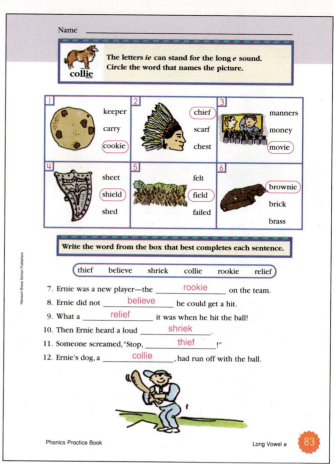
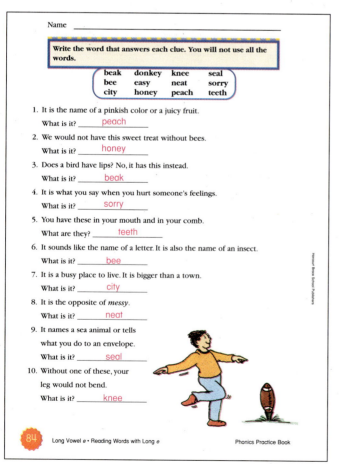

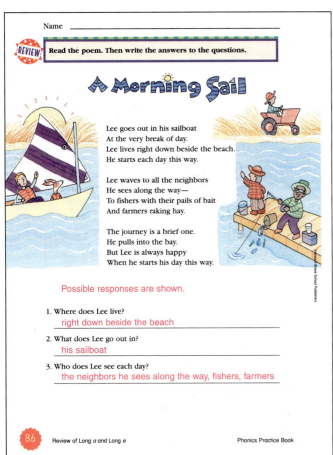
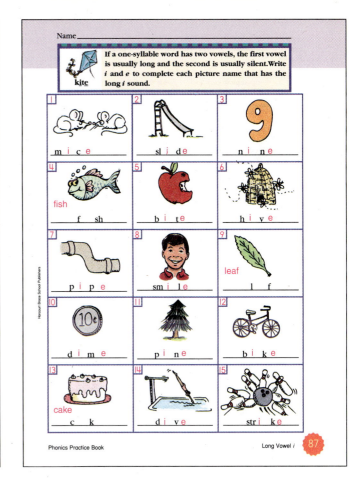
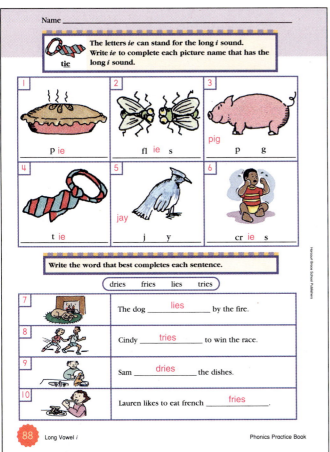
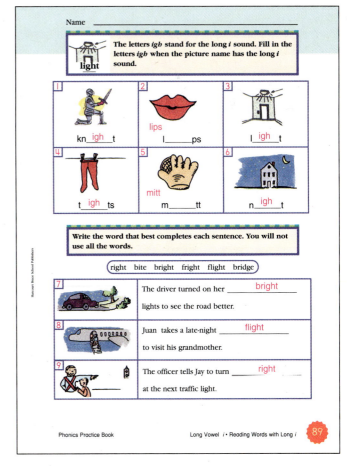

Phonics Practice Book Teacher's Edition 25

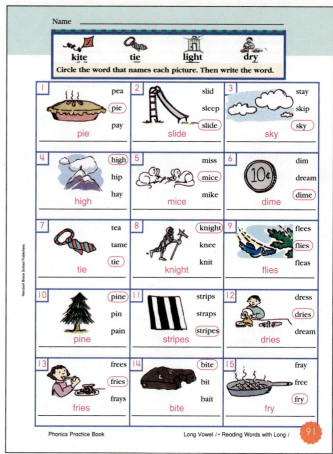
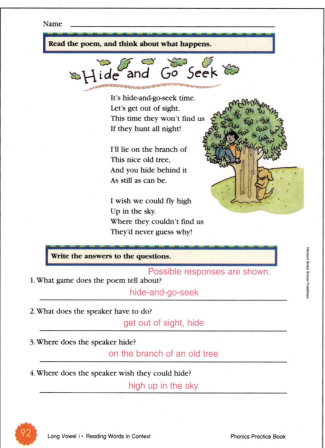

26

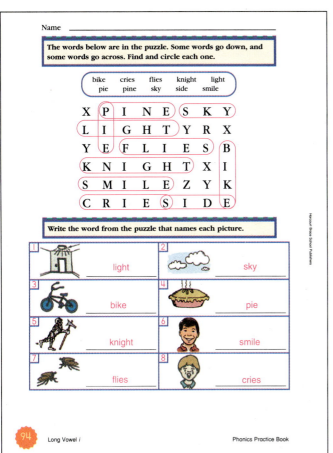

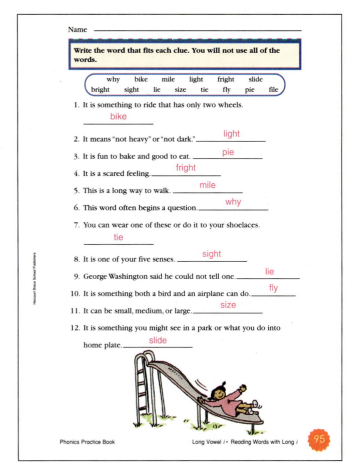

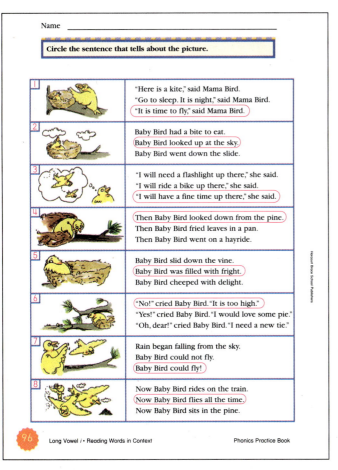

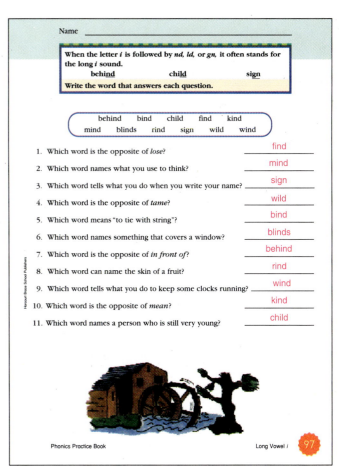

Phonics Practice Book Teacher's Edition   27

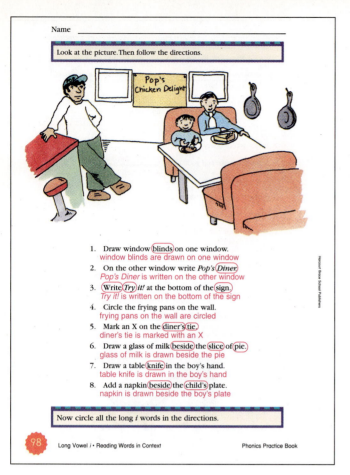

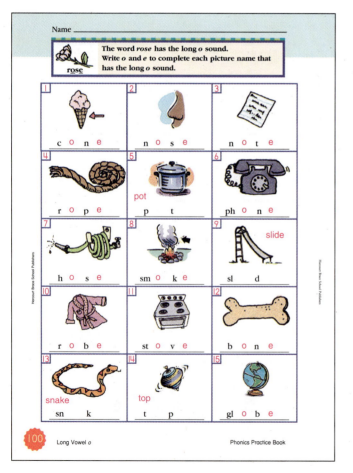

28   Phonics Practice Book Teacher's Edition

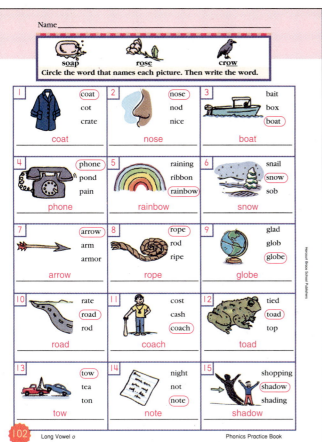

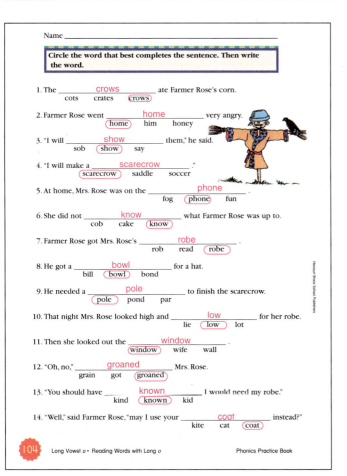

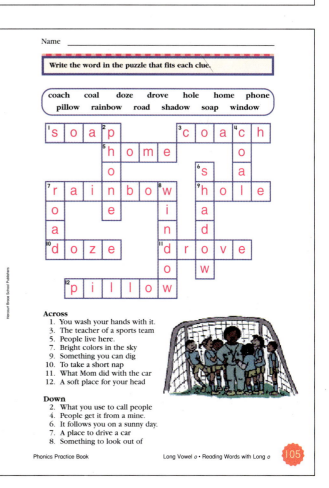

Page 106

Name _____

Write the word that fits each clue.

foal	rope	hole	slow	globe
low	mow	phone	oats	throne
float	woke	croak	roast	joke

1. You tell one to make people laugh. — joke
2. You can tie things up with this. — rope
3. When it rings, you pick it up. — phone
4. It is the sound a frog makes. — croak
5. You do this to food in your oven. — roast
6. This is something you can do in the water. — float
7. A horse thinks this is a treat. — oats
8. It is a map in the shape of the Earth. — globe
9. This is something you make when you dig. — hole
10. It is the opposite of *high*. — low
11. It is a chair for a king or a queen. — throne
12. It is the first thing you did this morning. — woke
13. It is something you do to grass. — mow
14. It is the opposite of *fast*. — slow
15. It is a name for a baby horse. — foal

106 — Long Vowel *o* • Reading Words with Long *o*

Page 107

Name _____

Circle the sentence that tells about the picture.

1. (Joan and Mom load up the car.)
   Joan and Mom get on their bikes.
   Joan and Mom are on the phone.
2. They see a rainbow in the snow.
   They float on their backs down the stream.
   (They go to the cove by the lake.)
3. They like to stay home.
   They eat ice-cream cones.
   (They get into the boat.)
4. They phone home from the park.
   (They row to the park.)
   They run up the slope.
5. (Mom ties the boat with a rope.)
   Mom floats away in the boat.
   Joan likes to jump rope.
6. (It looks as if they are all alone.)
   They put on their coats.
   They look at the globe.
7. Mom broke the rope.
   Mom cooks oats on the stove.
   (Soon smoke will rise from the fire.)
8. They dig a hole.
   (They roast hot dogs.)
   They pick a rose.

Long *o* • Reading Words in Context — 107

Page 108

Name _____

The letter *o* can stand for the long *o* sound. Write the word that names the picture.

yolk roll cold zero gold comb

1. cold
2. comb
3. gold
4. yolk
5. zero
6. roll

Write the word that best completes each sentence.

over colt fold go hold old

7. This ___old___ game is still fun to play.
8. Draw a ___colt___ without a tail.
9. Then ___fold___ a big scarf to make a blindfold.
10. Tie the blindfold ___over___ your eyes.
11. In your hand, ___hold___ the colt's tail.
12. Now ___go___ to the colt, and try to pin the tail to the right spot.

108 — Long Vowel *o* • Reading Words with Long *o*

Page 109

Name _____

Write the word that answers each clue.

bowl	elbow	note	rose
coat	grow	rainbow	show
code	hose	rope	slow

1. You can water a garden with it. ___hose___
2. You can jump with it or tie something with it. ___rope___
3. It is the name of a flower. ___rose___
4. It means "not fast." ___slow___
5. You wear one when it is cold outside. ___coat___
6. If the sun shines through rain, you may see one of these. ___rainbow___
7. It is a short letter or a part of a song. ___note___
8. Your address has a ZIP ___code___.
9. It is another name for a movie. ___show___
10. It is something you eat cereal and other foods out of. ___bowl___
11. A plant does it quickly. You do it too, but slowly. ___grow___
12. You can bend your arm because you have this. ___elbow___

Long *o* • Reading Words with Long *o* — 109

---

30   Phonics Practice Book Teacher's Edition

Name _____

Read the paragraphs and answer the questions.

SECRET CODES

Would you like to write a note to a friend that no one else can read? Then write your note in code!

Writing in code can be fun. Most codes could be broken. One United States code never was. It was a code made up by Navaho Indians and based on the Navaho speech. Navaho Marines spoke the code that helped the United States win a war.

There are many ways to make up your own codes. You can write your note backward, like this: .eert kao eht ta em teeM.

You can also make up a number code. For an easy number code, use 1 for *A*, 2 for *B*, and so on. This code is shown below:

1=A	2=B	3=C	4=D	5=E	6=F	7=G	8=H
9=I	10=J	11=K	12=L	13=M	14=N	15=O	
16=P	17=Q	18=R	19=S	20=T	21=U	22=V	
23=W	24=X	25=Y	26=Z				

Possible responses are shown.

1. Who made up a code that was never broken? **Navaho Indians**
2. Decode this message:

    14 15 23 / 25 15 21 / 11 14 15 23 / 1 12 12 /

    1 2 15 21 20 / 12 15 14 7 / 15.

    Now you know all about long *o*.

Name _____

Circle the letter or letters that stand for the long vowel sound in the picture name. Then write the word.

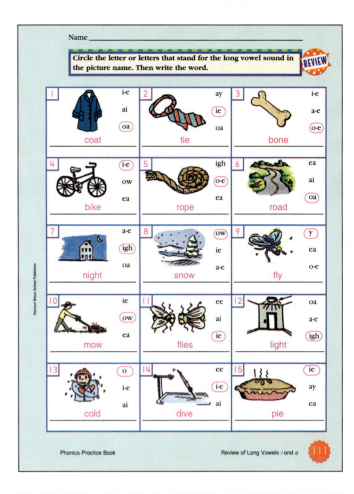

Name _____

Read the poem. Then write the answers to the questions.

Showtime at the Fair

Di will show her new colt.
Joan will show her pet goat.
Joe's fine golden duckling
Will dive and float.

Bo has baby chicks
That cannot fly high.
They hide behind Mother Hen
Tiny and shy.

I ride a white pony
Just right for my size.
Oh, here come the judges—
Hope I win a prize!

Possible responses are shown.

1. What will Di and Joan show?
    a colt and a goat

2. What do the baby chicks do?
    hide behind the mother hen

3. What will the judges do?
    They will give out prizes.

4. What pet will the speaker of the poem show?
    A white pony just right for her size.

Name _____

The word *mule* has the long *u* sound. Write the letters *u* and *e* to complete each picture name that has the long *u* sound.

Phonics Practice Book Teacher's Edition

31

Name _____

Read the poem. Then write the answers to the questions.

Come march to our tune.
Bring your flute to play.
We're going to have
A parade today.

We'll wear uniforms
And hats with plumes,
While some twirl batons
In cute costumes.

Possible responses are shown.

1. What are the children going to do?
   march to the tune; bring a flute to play

2. What does the speaker invite a friend to do?
   join the parade

3. What would be a good title for the poem?
   Responses will vary.

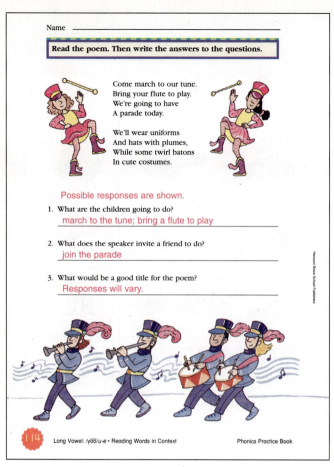

114   Long Vowel: /yōō/u-e • Reading Words in Context   Phonics Practice Book

---

Name _____

Circle the word that best completes the sentence. Then write the word.

1. Try not to be ___rude___.
   red   (rude)   run

2. Push toothpaste from the bottom of the ___tube___.
   tab   tub   (tube)

3. Don't ___refuse___ to share.
   recall   reef   (refuse)

4. Don't ___pollute___ the Earth with litter.
   (pollute)   pillow   polo

5. Be kind to animals, even ___mules___.
   miles   (mules)   mugs

6. Say thank you if someone says you're ___cute___.
   curl   (cute)   cutter

7. Try to follow the ___tune___ when you sing.
   (tune)   ton   tulip

8. Chewing ice ___cubes___ may break a tooth.
   canes   (cubes)   cubs

9. Throw your dirty clothes in the laundry ___chute___.
   shut   chain   (chute)

10. Keep the ___volume___ down on your radio.
    valley   (volume)   very

11. Don't ___use___ your brother's toys.
    (use)   as   us

12. Don't make too many ___rules___.
    (rules)   rolls   rails

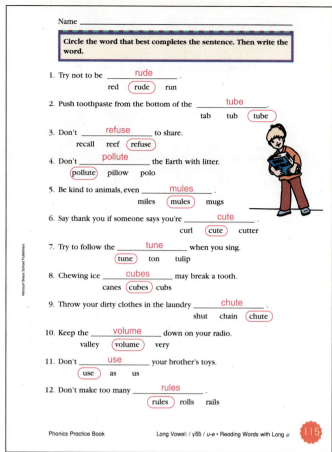

Phonics Practice Book   Long Vowel: /yōō/u-e • Reading Words with Long u   115

Name _____

The words below are in the puzzle. Some words go down. Some words go across. Find and circle each one.

chute   cube   dune   flute   June   mule
plume   pollute   tube   tune   cute

X	A	R	F	T	H	I	C
P	O	L	L	U	T	E	H
L	I	C	U	B	E	J	U
U	C	U	T	E	Z	U	T
M	U	L	E	T	U	N	E
E	Z	D	U	N	E	E	U

Write the word from the puzzle that names each picture. You will not use all of the words.

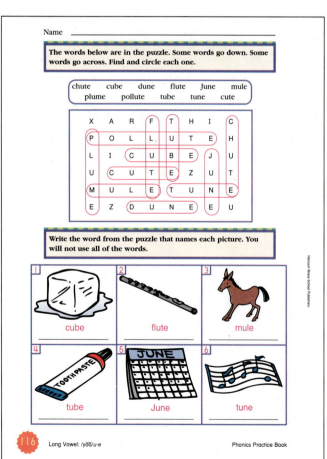

1. cube
2. flute
3. mule
4. tube
5. June
6. tune

116   Long Vowel: /yōō/u-e   Phonics Practice Book

Name _____

Write the word that fits each clue.

tune   cube   parachute   June   mule   flute
plume   huge   costume   cute   spruce   pollute

1. It is an animal that is like a horse. ___mule___
2. It is the opposite of tiny. ___huge___
3. People play pretty music on this. ___flute___
4. It is a month of the year. ___June___
5. It is the feather on a hat. ___plume___
6. It's what people say babies are. ___cute___
7. Our planet will stay clean if we don't do this. ___pollute___
8. You can play or sing this. ___tune___
9. You may wear this if you act in a play. ___costume___
10. It is a kind of tree. ___spruce___
11. You'd better wear this if you jump out of a plane. ___parachute___
12. It is a word for a square piece of ice. ___cube___

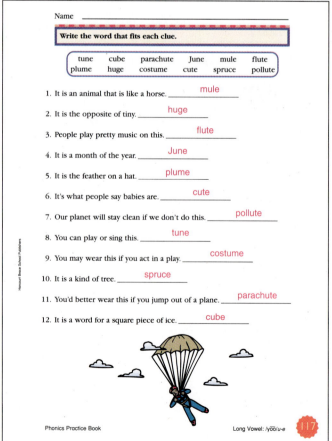

Phonics Practice Book   Long Vowel: /yōō/u-e   117

---

32   Phonics Practice Book Teacher's Edition

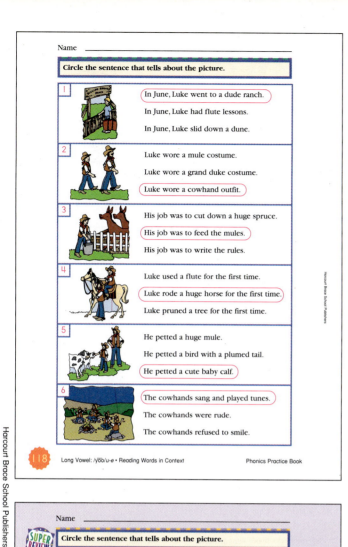
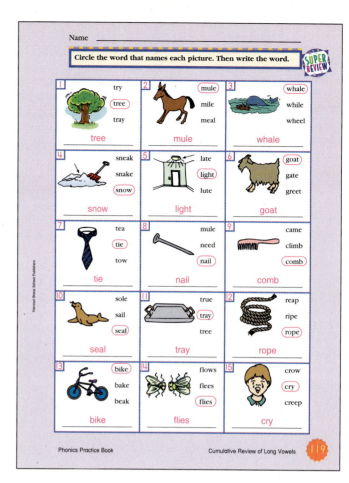
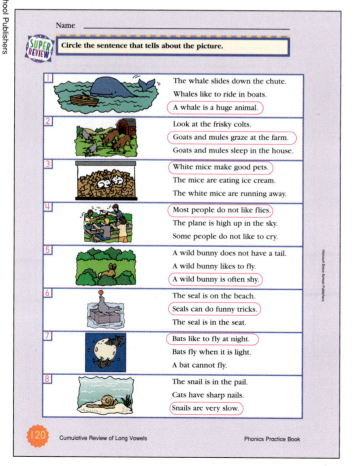
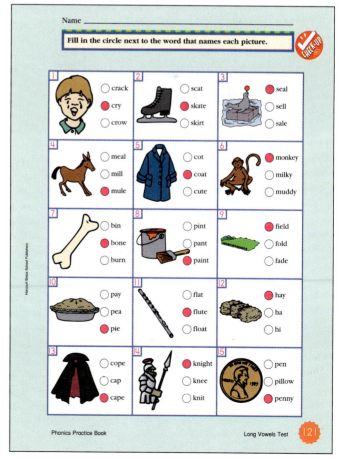

Phonics Practice Book Teacher's Edition

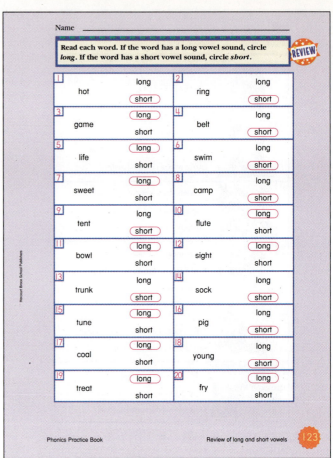

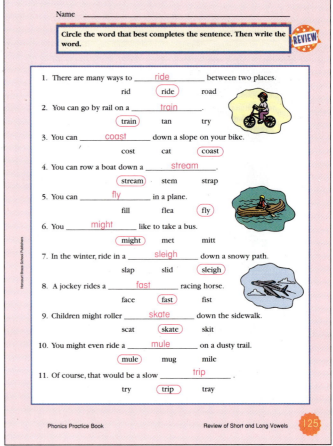

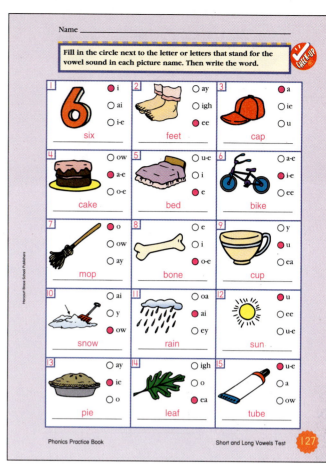
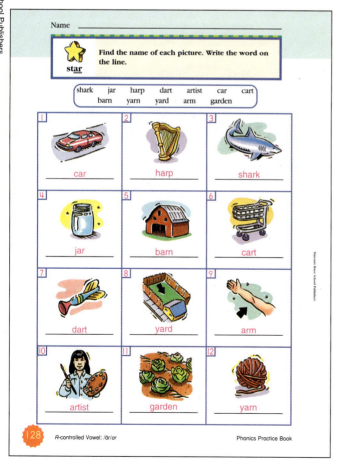
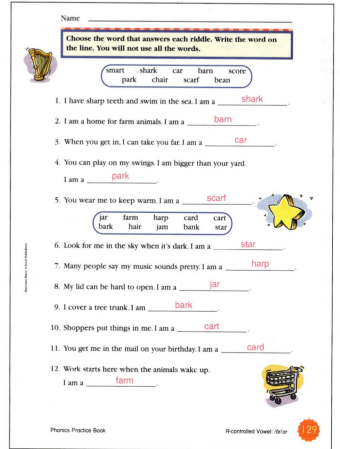

Phonics Practice Book Teacher's Edition

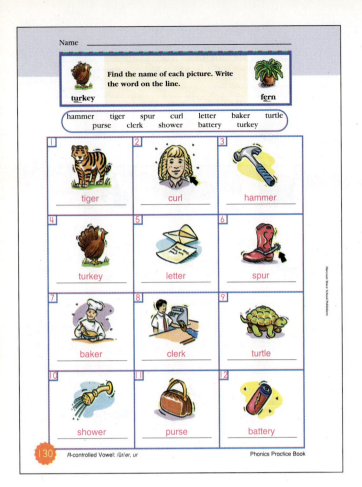

Page 130 — Find the name of each picture. Write the word on the line. (turkey, fern)

Word box: hammer, tiger, spur, curl, letter, baker, turtle, purse, clerk, shower, battery, turkey

1. tiger
2. curl
3. hammer
4. turkey
5. letter
6. spur
7. baker
8. clerk
9. turtle
10. shower
11. purse
12. battery

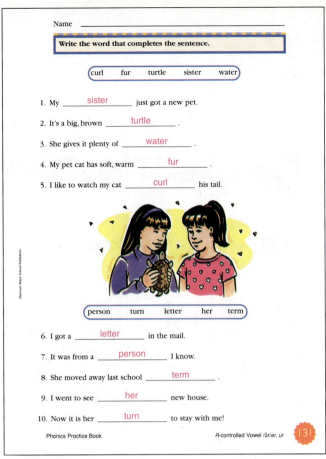

Page 131 — Write the word that completes the sentence.

Word box: curl, fur, turtle, sister, water

1. My **sister** just got a new pet.
2. It's a big, brown **turtle**.
3. She gives it plenty of **water**.
4. My pet cat has soft, warm **fur**.
5. I like to watch my cat **curl** his tail.

Word box: person, turn, letter, her, term

6. I got a **letter** in the mail.
7. It was from a **person** I know.
8. She moved away last school **term**.
9. I went to see **her** new house.
10. Now it is her **turn** to stay with me!

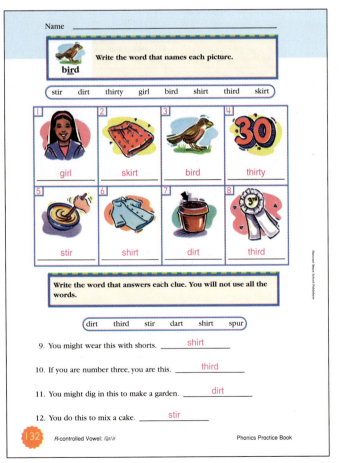

Page 132 — Write the word that names each picture. (bird)

Word box: stir, dirt, thirty, girl, bird, shirt, third, skirt

1. girl
2. skirt
3. bird
4. thirty
5. stir
6. shirt
7. dirt
8. third

Write the word that answers each clue. You will not use all the words.

Word box: dirt, third, stir, dart, shirt, spur

9. You might wear this with shorts. **shirt**
10. If you are number three, you are this. **third**
11. You might dig in this to make a garden. **dirt**
12. You do this to mix a cake. **stir**

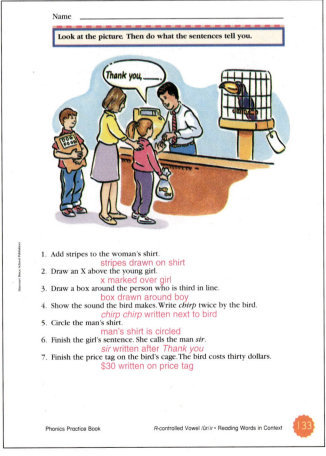

Page 133 — Look at the picture. Then do what the sentences tell you.

1. Add stripes to the woman's shirt. *stripes drawn on shirt*
2. Draw an X above the young girl. *x marked over girl*
3. Draw a box around the person who is third in line. *box drawn around boy*
4. Show the sound the bird makes. Write *chirp* twice by the bird. *chirp chirp written next to bird*
5. Circle the man's shirt. *man's shirt is circled*
6. Finish the girl's sentence. She calls the man *sir*. *sir written after Thank you*
7. Finish the price tag on the bird's cage. The bird costs thirty dollars. *$30 written on price tag*

Phonics Practice Book Teacher's Edition

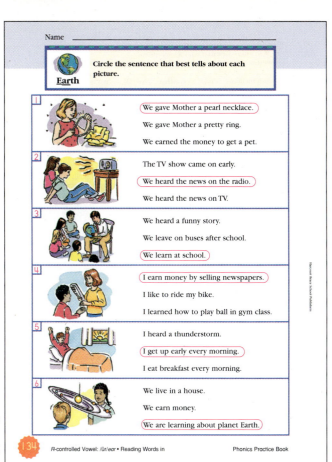
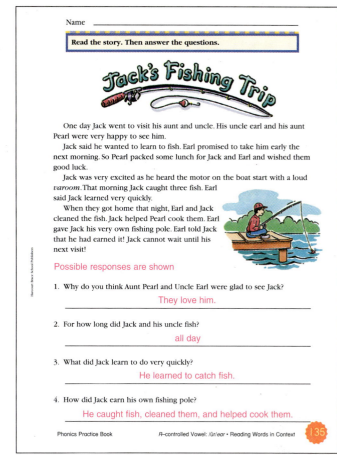
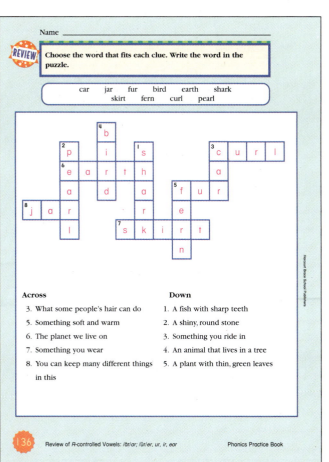
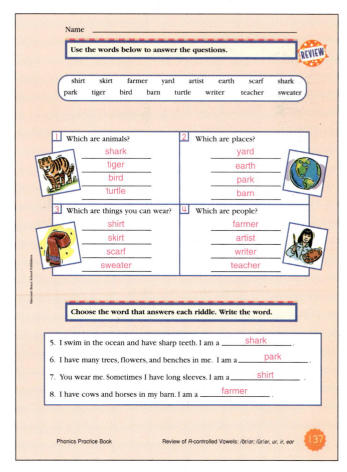

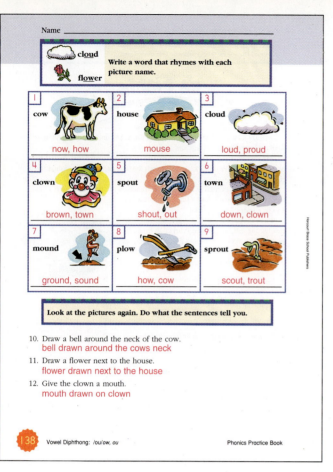
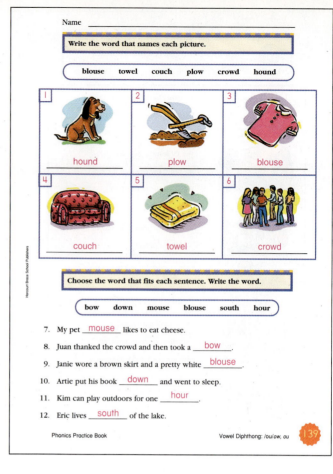
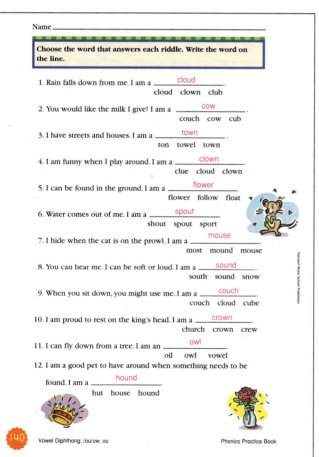
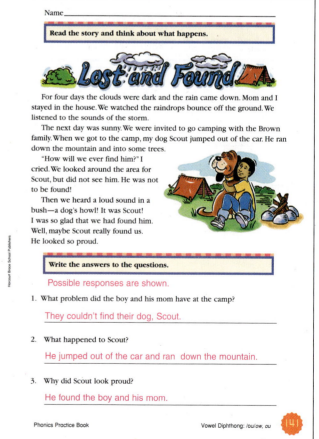

38

Phonics Practice Book Teacher's Edition

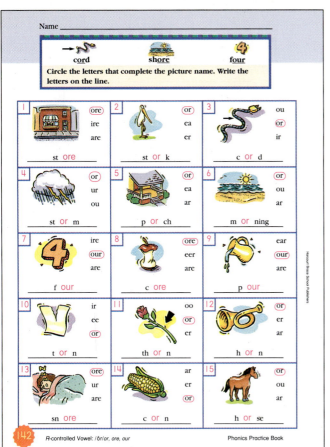
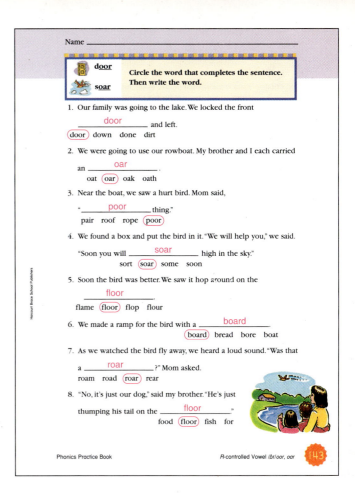
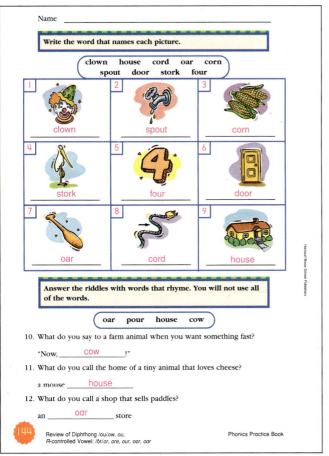
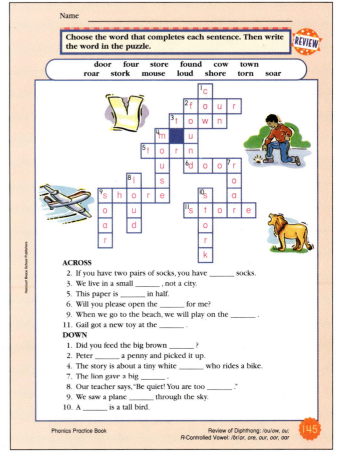

Phonics Practice Book Teacher's Edition

39

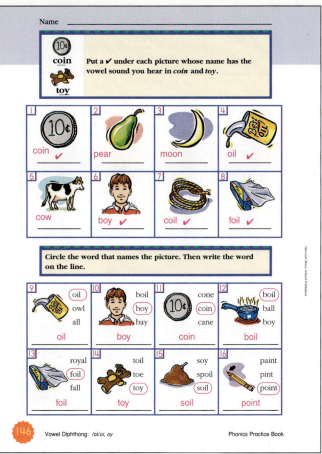

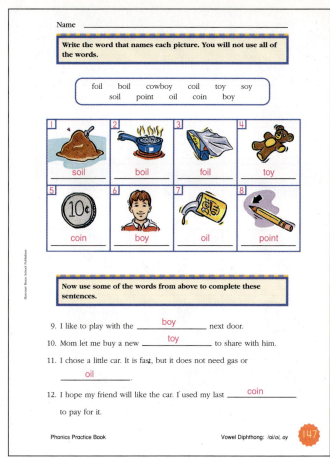
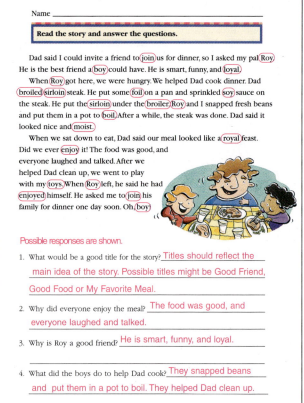

40 Phonics Practice Book Teacher's Edition

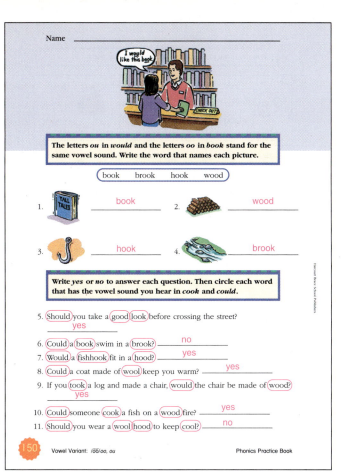

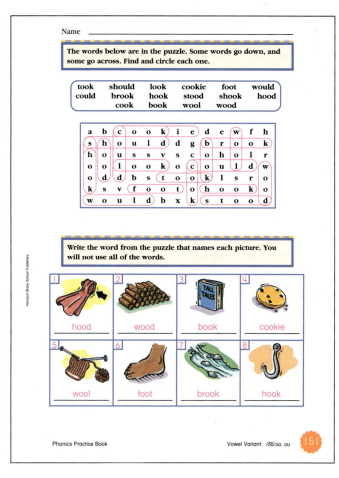

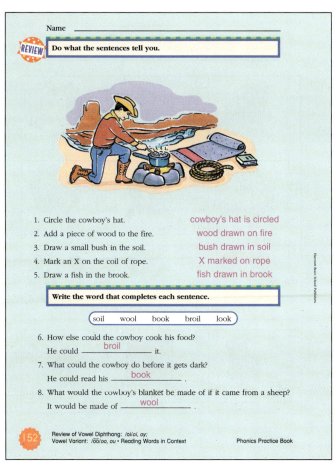

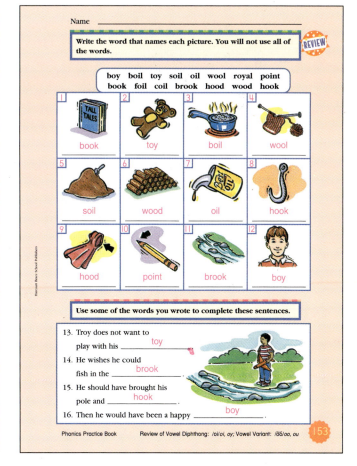

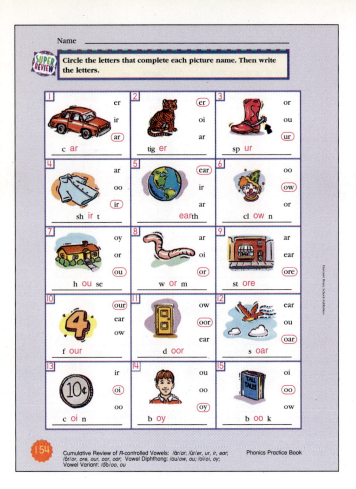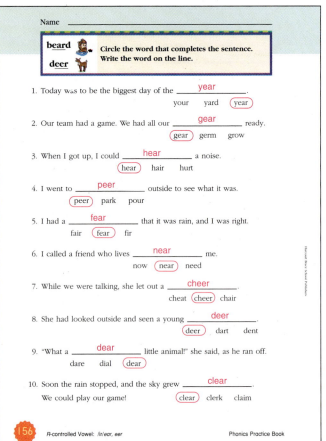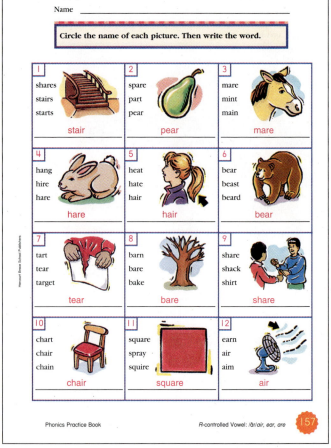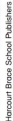

42 Phonics Practice Book Teacher's Edition

Name _____

Read the story and think about what happens.

We have pear trees on our farm. In the winter the trees are bare. In the spring they have flowers that make the air smell nice. In the summer the trees are full of pears. When the trees have pears, my friend and I help pick them.

We get up on chairs to reach the pears. We pick all we can reach. I save a few for Clair, my mare. My friend gives some to his pet hare, Carey. We walk back to the house and sit on the stairs to eat our good, sweet pears.

Write the answers to the questions.

1. What would be a good title for the story?
   Responses will vary.
2. How do the trees change during the year?
   In the winter they are bare; in the spring they have flowers;
   in the summer they have pears.
3. Who eats the pears?
   the children, the mare, the pet hare

158 R-controlled Vowel: /âr/air, ear, are • Reading Words in Context   Phonics Practice Book

---

Name _____

Read the sentences and do what they tell you. REVIEW

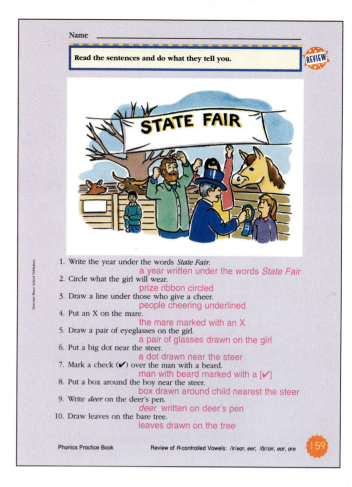

1. Write the year under the words *State Fair*.
   a year written under the words *State Fair*
2. Circle what the girl will wear.
   prize ribbon circled
3. Draw a line under those who give a cheer.
   people cheering underlined
4. Put an X on the mare.
   the mare marked with an X
5. Draw a pair of eyeglasses on the girl.
   a pair of glasses drawn on the girl
6. Put a big dot near the steer.
   a dot drawn near the steer
7. Mark a check (✔) over the man with a beard.
   man with beard marked with a [✔]
8. Put a box around the boy near the steer.
   box drawn around child nearest the steer
9. Write *deer* on the deer's pen.
   deer written on deer's pen
10. Draw leaves on the bare tree.
    leaves drawn on the tree

Phonics Practice Book   Review of *R*-controlled Vowels: /ir/ear, eer, /âr/air, ear, are   159

Name _____

REVIEW **Read the poem, and answer the questions.**

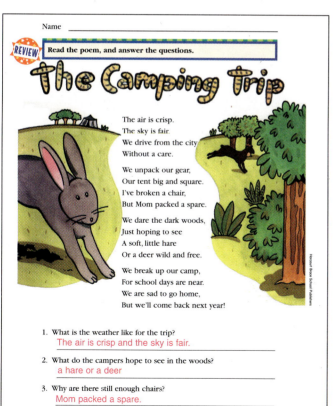

The Camping Trip

The air is crisp.
The sky is fair.
We drive from the city
Without a care.

We unpack our gear,
Our tent big and square.
I've broken a chair,
But Mom packed a spare.

We dare the dark woods,
Just hoping to see
A soft, little hare
Or a deer wild and free.

We break up our camp,
For school days are near.
We are sad to go home,
But we'll come back next year!

1. What is the weather like for the trip?
   The air is crisp and the sky is fair.
2. What do the campers hope to see in the woods?
   a hare or a deer
3. Why are there still enough chairs?
   Mom packed a spare.

160 Review of R-controlled Vowels: /ir/ ear, eer, /âr/ air, ear,   Phonics Practice Book

---

Name _____

 flew
blue

Write an *ew* or a *ue* word to answer each question.

1. What is a color that rhymes with *glue*? ___blue___
2. What can help you solve a mystery? It rhymes with *true*.
   ___clue___
3. What word tells what you do to your food and rhymes with *threw*?
   ___chew___
4. What can you eat with a spoon that rhymes with *few*?
   ___stew___
5. What do you call a team of people who work together?
   with *grew*. ___crew___

Complete each sentence with an *ew* or *ue* word.

6. My sister lost her ring. She did not have a ___clue___ where to find it.
7. She said, "I had it when I was helping Dad make ___stew___ for supper."
8. "Maybe you threw it out with the peels in the ___blue___ trash bag," I said.
9. "That must be it!" she said. We ran home to check the bag before the garbage ___crew___ picked it up.

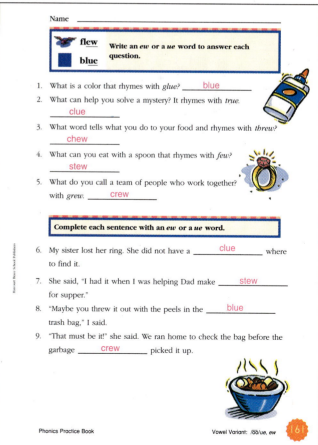

Phonics Practice Book   Vowel Variant: /o͞o/ue, ew   161

Phonics Practice Book Teacher's Edition   43

Name _____

Circle the word that answers each riddle. Write the word on the line.

1. I am the color of the sky on a bright, clear day. I am ___blue___.
   bloom (blue) blank

2. When you do not know something, I help you find it out. I am a ___clue___.
   chew (clue) coop

3. I am a boy, and I have an aunt. I am her ___nephew___.
   (nephew) noon next

4. I make things stick to paper. I am ___glue___.
   glare gleam (glue)

5. You can walk down me because I am like a street. I am an ___avenue___.
   afternoon (avenue) animal

6. I am a special kind of stone you can wear. I am a ___jewel___.
   (jewel) jeep juice

7. I am a thick soup with carrots, potatoes, and meat. I am a ___stew___.
   (stew) stool street

8. When you read me, I tell you about things that have happened. I am the ___news___.
   near (news) noise

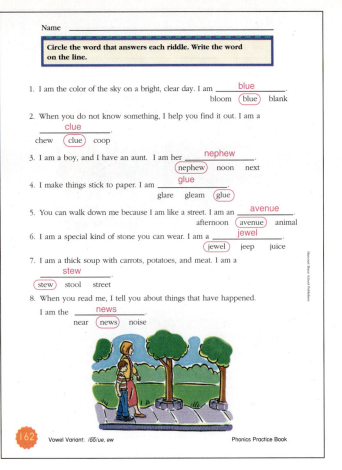

Vowel Variant: /o͞o/ue, ew • Phonics Practice Book 162

Name _____

Read the book titles. Look for words that have the vowel sound you hear in the words *grew* and *glue*. Then write the words under the correct heading.

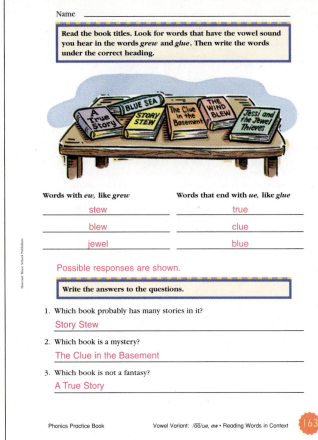

Words with *ew*, like *grew*	Words that end with *ue*, like *glue*
stew	true
blew	clue
jewel	blue

Possible responses are shown.

Write the answers to the questions.

1. Which book probably has many stories in it?
   Story Stew

2. Which book is a mystery?
   The Clue in the Basement

3. Which book is not a fantasy?
   A True Story

Vowel Variant: /o͞o/ue, ew • Reading Words in Context 163

Name _____

Read the story and think about what happens.

When I Flew to Aunt Sue's

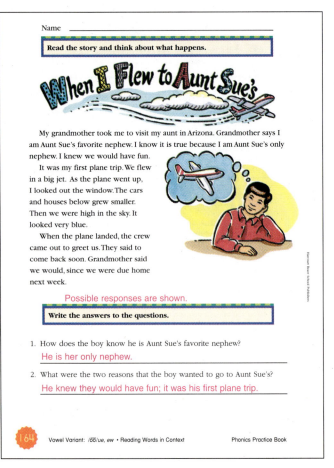

My grandmother took me to visit my aunt in Arizona. Grandmother says I am Aunt Sue's favorite nephew. I know it is true because I am Aunt Sue's only nephew. I knew we would have fun.

It was my first plane trip. We flew in a big jet. As the plane went up, I looked out the window. The cars and houses below grew smaller. Then we were high in the sky. It looked very blue.

When the plane landed, the crew came out to greet us. They said to come back soon. Grandmother said we would, since we were due home next week.

Possible responses are shown.

Write the answers to the questions.

1. How does the boy know he is Aunt Sue's favorite nephew?
   He is her only nephew.

2. What were the two reasons that the boy wanted to go to Aunt Sue's?
   He knew they would have fun; it was his first plane trip.

Vowel Variant: /o͞o/ue, ew • Reading Words in Context 164

Name _____

🌙 moon **Write the word from the box that names the picture.**

| igloo | goose | boot | broom |
| stool | spoon | roof | kangaroo |

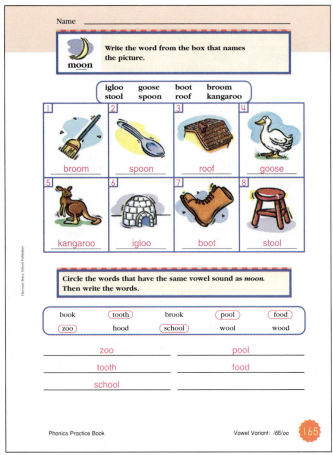

1. broom
2. spoon
3. roof
4. goose
5. kangaroo
6. igloo
7. boot
8. stool

Circle the words that have the same vowel sound as *moon*. Then write the words.

book (tooth) brook (pool) (food)
(zoo) hood (school) wool wood

zoo   pool
tooth   food
school

Vowel Variant: /o͞o/oo 165

44

Phonics Practice Book Teacher's Edition

Name _____

Read the story and think about what happens.

Scouts in the Afternoon

All day at school, I was in a good mood. I knew that in the afternoon I would meet with my scout troop at the park. Our leader, Ms. Moon, would read to us from our scout book. Then we would pick up trash and take turns sweeping the sidewalk with a broom. Later we might shoot some hoops. Ms. Moon might even take us for a swim in the pool. One time she took us to the zoo.

Then we would have a snack. I brought the food. My mom and I made cookies. I knew those cookies were good. Everyone in my troop has a sweet tooth! The afternoon could not come too soon!

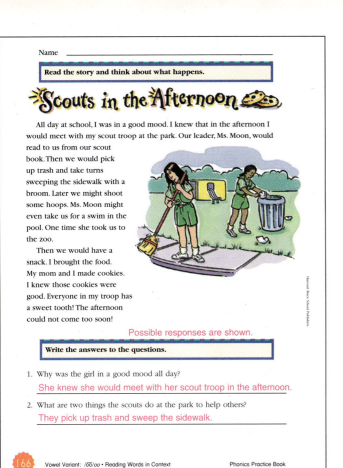

Possible responses are shown.

Write the answers to the questions.

1. Why was the girl in a good mood all day?
   She knew she would meet with her scout troop in the afternoon.
2. What are two things the scouts do at the park to help others?
   They pick up trash and sweep the sidewalk.

166 Vowel Variant: /ōō/oo • Reading Words in Context   Phonics Practice Book

---

Name _____

soup
fruit

Circle the word that fits the clue.

1. It is a black-and-blue mark on your skin.
   brook   (bruise)   buses
2. You use a spoon to eat this.
   (soup)   soon   sew
3. It is a trip you take on a ship.
   crew   cool   (cruise)
4. It is a large member of the cat family.
   coop   (cougar)   could
5. Lemons, apples, and pears are this.
   fright   frisky   (fruit)
6. This can be a matching jacket and pants.
   (suit)   soup   sure
7. You might drink this in the morning.
   jewel   junk   (juice)
8. This tells about more than one.
   grew   gloom   (group)

Look at the words you circled. Can you find three pairs of rhyming words? Write them on the lines below.

-oup	-uit	-uise
soup	suit	cruise
group	fruit	bruise

Phonics Practice Book   Vowel Variant: /ōō/ou, ui   167

Name _____

REVIEW — Circle the sentence that tells about the picture.

1. (Drew stirs the soup with a big spoon.)
   Drew steers the spaceship to the moon.
   Drew shoots the ball through the hoop.

2. Drew says the moon will be out soon.
   (Drew says the soup will be done at noon.)
   Drew says he needs a new tool.

3. Sue will fix the screw.
   Sue will join the crew.
   (Sue will sit on a stool.)

4. They have to look for their jewels.
   (They have to let their soup cool.)
   They have to see how much they grew.

5. Drew will help Sue blow up the balloon.
   (Drew will help Sue clean up the room.)
   Drew will help Sue look for the clue.

6. (Drew sweeps with the broom.)
   Drew has a good time at the zoo.
   Drew has a big, blue bruise.

168 Review of Vowel Variant: /ōō/ue, ew, oo, ou, ui   Phonics Practice Book

---

Name _____

REVIEW — Use words from the box to answer the questions.

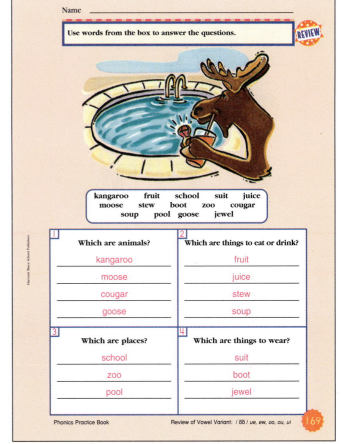

kangaroo	fruit	school	suit	juice
moose	stew	boot	zoo	cougar
soup	pool	goose	jewel	

1. **Which are animals?**
   kangaroo
   moose
   cougar
   goose

2. **Which are things to eat or drink?**
   fruit
   juice
   stew
   soup

3. **Which are places?**
   school
   zoo
   pool

4. **Which are things to wear?**
   suit
   boot
   jewel

Phonics Practice Book   Review of Vowel Variant: /ōō/ue, ew, oo, ou, ui   169

Phonics Practice Book Teacher's Edition   45

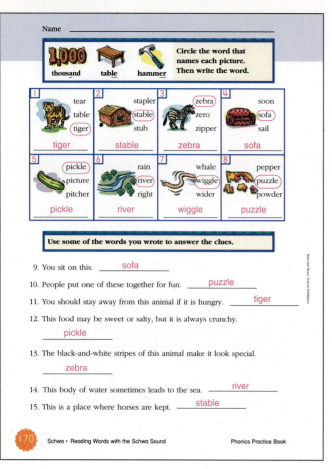

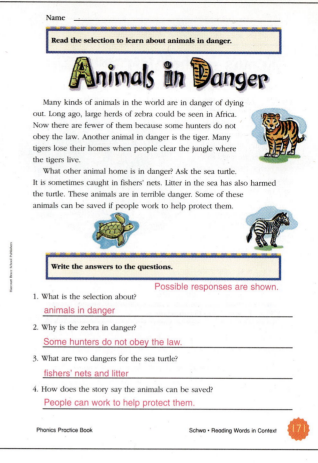

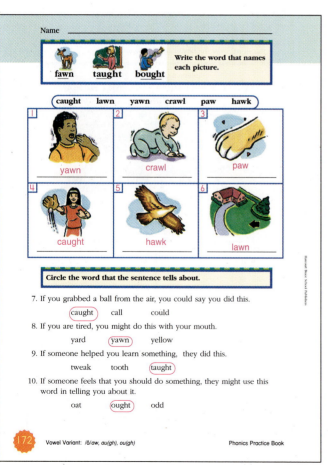

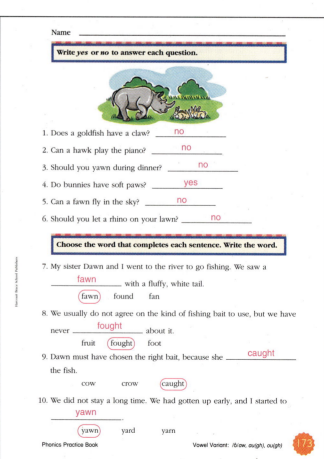

46

Name _____

Read the story, and think about what happens.

Grandpa and I got up at dawn and went into the woods. We wanted to see some animals. We thought we might see some birds and a few squirrels. Were we ever surprised by what we saw!

When we sat down for a rest, I saw something moving in the trees. I was not sure what it was. Then I knew. It was a bear! It had long, sharp claws, and big, strong jaws. I told Grandpa we ought to go. Just then, the bear ran away. Was I ever glad! That bear taught me that I ought to be careful when I'm in the woods.

Write the answers to the questions.

Possible responses are shown.

1. Why did the boy and his grandpa go into the woods?
   They wanted to see some animals.

2. What surprising thing did they see?
   a bear

3. What happened that made the boy glad?
   The bear ran away.

174 Vowel Variant: /ô/aw, augh, ough • Reading Words in Context   Phonics Practice Book

---

Name _____

Look at the picture. Then follow the directions.

1. Circle the person who is learning to crawl.
   baby is circled
2. The baby has just caught a ball. Draw the ball in his hands.
   ball is drawn in the baby's hands
3. Draw a line under the person who has taught the baby to catch.
   line is drawn under the mother
4. Finish the mother's thought.
   caught is written in the thought bubble
5. Put an X on the new thing the mother bought for the baby.
   an X is drawn on the new suit
6. Circle the thing the mother ought to give the baby when he is hungry.
   bottle is circled
7. Draw a pillow in the place where the mother will put the baby when he begins to yawn.
   pillow is drawn in the crib
8. Circle the puppy's paws. *dog's paws are circled*
9. Draw a window in the room that shows the front lawn.
   window showing the lawn is drawn

Phonics Practice Book   Vowel Variant: /ô/aw, au(gh), ou(gh) • Reading Words in Context   175

Name _____

REVIEW Write the word that names each picture.

bought	crawl	caught	hammer	taught
zipper	salad	fawn	table	thousand
sofa	thought	straw	puzzle	butter

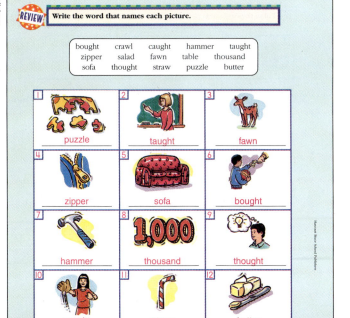

1. puzzle   2. taught   3. fawn
4. zipper   5. sofa   6. bought
7. hammer   8. thousand   9. thought
10. caught   11. straw   12. butter
13. table   14. salad   15. crawl

176   Review: Schwa; Vowel Variant: /ô/aw, au(gh), ou(gh)   Phonics Practice Book

---

Name _____

Use the rhyming words to complete the poem. Then answer the questions. **REVIEW**

| caught | stronger | thought | able |
| taught | ago | crawl | |

1. Have you ever heard the fable about the turtle who was ___*able*___?

2. Very, very long ___*ago*___, Turtle and Hare's race was the show.

3. Hare said speediness can't be ___*taught*___, it can't be promised or be bought.

4. But Turtle did not give up at all and moved along at a steady ___*crawl*___.

5. "Since I have time, I think I ought to take a nap right here," Hare ___*thought*___.

6. Turtle kept it up much longer and proved that he was really ___*stronger*___.

7. In the end, Hare had been taught that Turtle now could not be ___*caught*___!

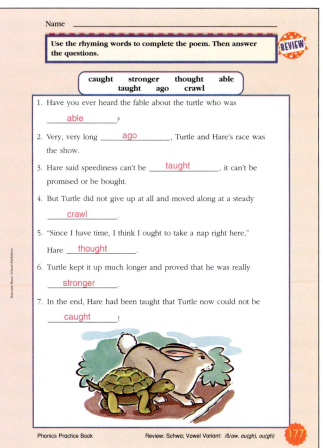

Phonics Practice Book   Review: Schwa; Vowel Variant: /ô/aw, au(gh), ou(gh)   177

Phonics Practice Book Teacher's Edition   47

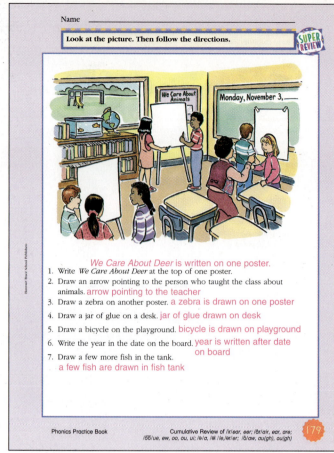

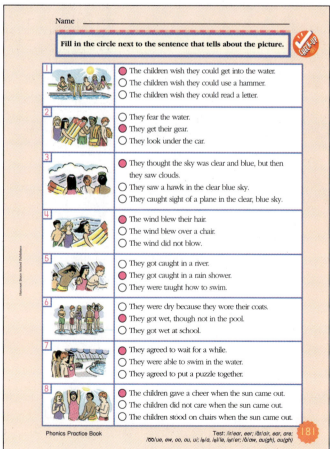

48 Phonics Practice Book Teacher's Edition

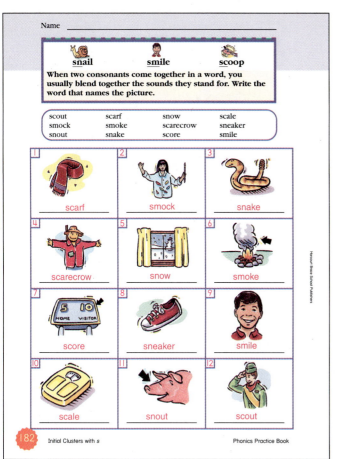
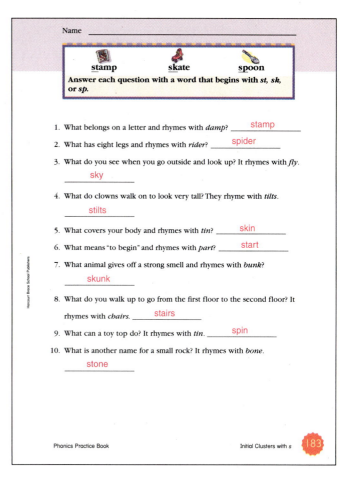
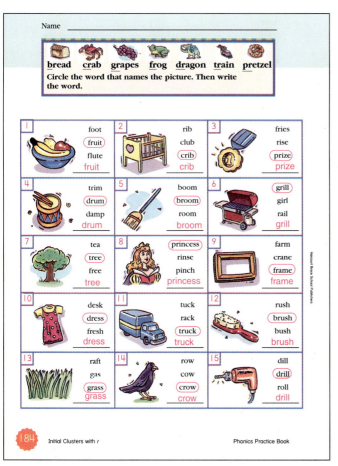
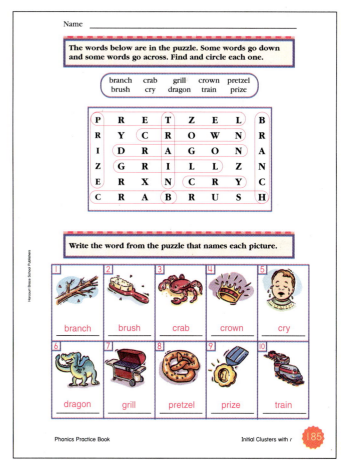

Phonics Practice Book Teacher's Edition

49

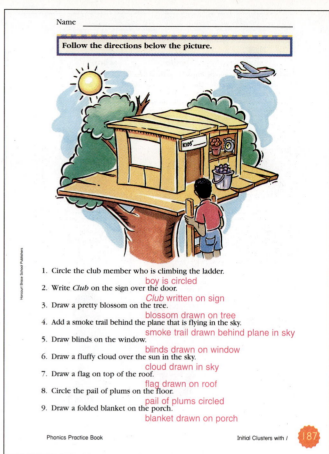
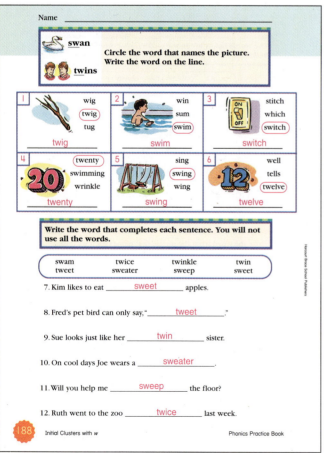
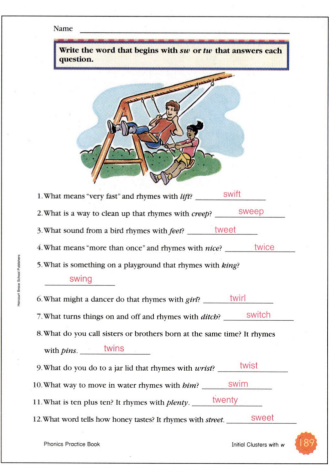

50

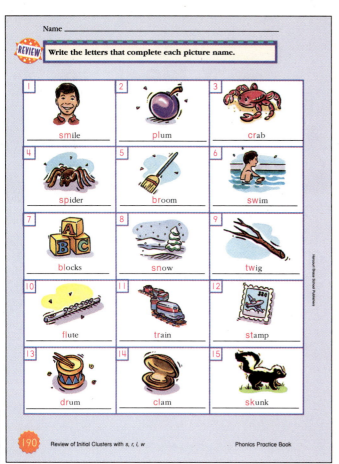
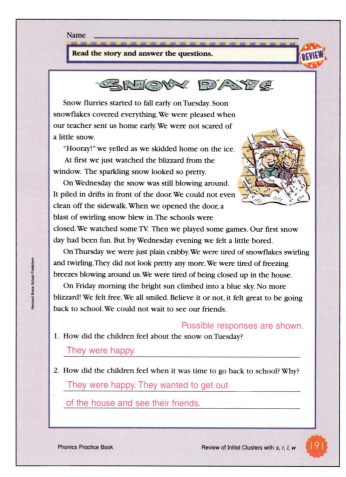
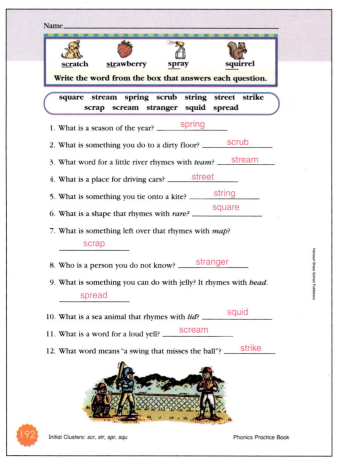
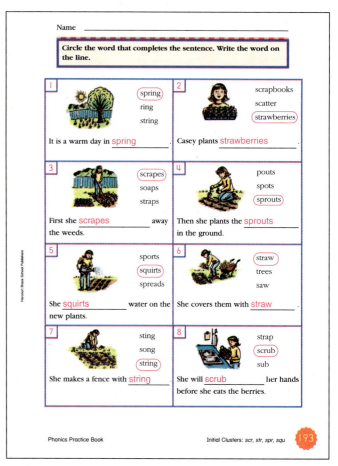

Phonics Practice Book Teacher's Edition

51

Name _____

Follow the directions. Write the new word. Then draw a picture of it.

1	Start with *wash*. Change *w* to *squ*.	squash	Drawings will vary.
2	Start with *wipe*. Change *w* to *str*.	stripe	
3	Start with *green*. Change the *gr* to *scr*.	screen	
4	Start with *hare*. Change *h* to *squ*.	square	
5	Start with *sing*. Change *s* to *spr*.	spring	
6	Start with *bring*. Change *br* to *str*.	string	

194 Initial Clusters: *scr, str, spr, squ*

Name _____

Read the poem. Then write the answers to the questions.

The Big Game

We sprint to the field.
The crowd gives a scream.
We are strong, we are mighty—
The number one team.

We spring up so high
To catch every ball.
We watch the other team—
Squirm, squeal, and sprawl.

By the end of the game,
We're scruffy and dirty,
But we feel no stress—
The score is zero to thirty.

Bright streamers are flying.
Winning is fun!
We've stretched out our streak
And are still number ONE!

Possible responses are shown.

1. How do the players feel at the end of the game? Why?
   They are happy because they are still number one.

2. Write a headline about the game for the team scrapbook.
   Responses will vary. Possible answer is: Number one team wins again!

Initial Clusters: *scr, str, spr, squ* • Reading Words in Context 195

Name _____

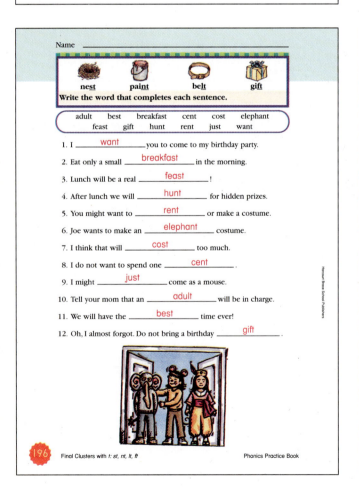

nest   paint   belt   gift

Write the word that completes each sentence.

| adult | best | breakfast | cent | cost | elephant |
| feast | gift | hunt | rent | just | want |

1. I ___want___ you to come to my birthday party.
2. Eat only a small ___breakfast___ in the morning.
3. Lunch will be a real ___feast___!
4. After lunch we will ___hunt___ for hidden prizes.
5. You might want to ___rent___ or make a costume.
6. Joe wants to make an ___elephant___ costume.
7. I think that will ___cost___ too much.
8. I do not want to spend one ___cent___.
9. I might ___just___ come as a mouse.
10. Tell your mom that an ___adult___ will be in charge.
11. We will have the ___best___ time ever!
12. Oh, I almost forgot. Do not bring a birthday ___gift___.

196 Final Clusters with *t: st, nt, lt, ft*

Name _____

Circle the word that fits the clue.

1. You eat this in the morning.
   bolt   (breakfast)   bent
2. This can be used to lock your door.
   bush   (bolt)   ball
3. You do this with a pencil to make letters or words.
   pest   prize   (print)
4. This means a pile of snow blown by the wind.
   drill   (drift)   dent
5. This is a horse's baby.
   cold   (colt)   cart
6. This means "the land next to an ocean."
   (coast)   coat   cone
7. This is the opposite of right.
   list   laugh   (left)
8. This often goes with pepper.
   sift   sail   (salt)
9. This has a trunk but never packs it.
   eleven   telephone   (elephant)
10. You may do this to a cake after you bake it.
    (frost)   fish   flat
11. This is something you might float on in a lake.
    (raft)   rent   roof
12. This is not the back.
    from   (front)   frog

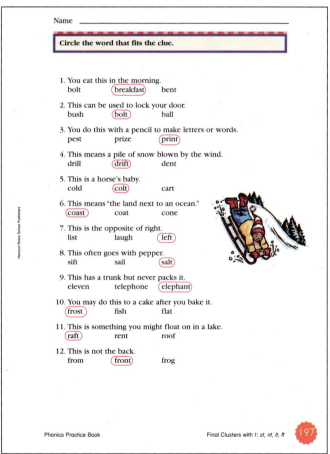

Final Clusters with *t: st, nt, lt, ft* 197

---

52   Phonics Practice Book Teacher's Edition

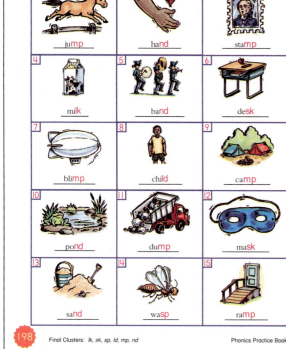
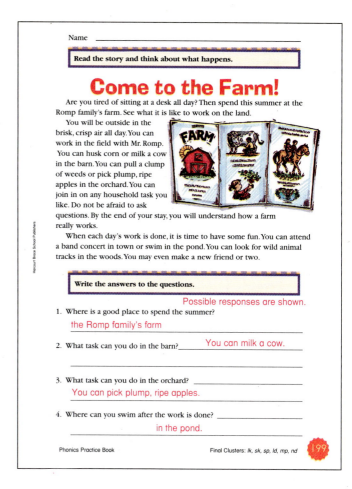
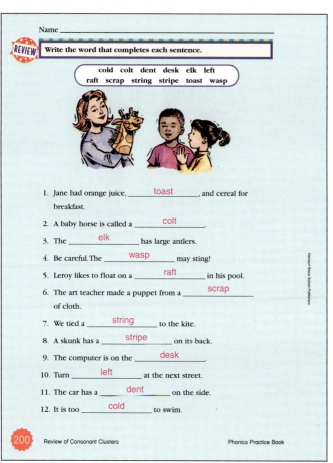
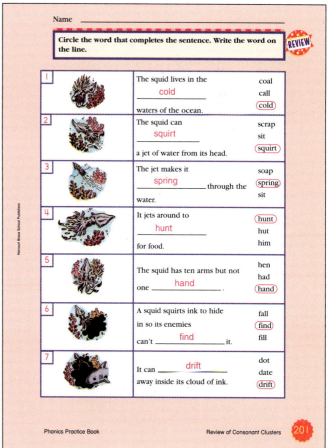

Phonics Practice Book Teacher's Edition

53

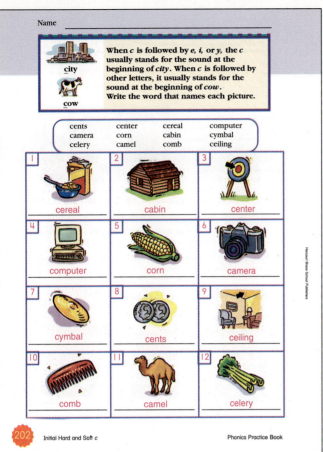

Page 202 — Initial Hard and Soft c

Name _____

When *c* is followed by *e*, *i*, or *y*, the *c* usually stands for the sound at the beginning of *city*. When *c* is followed by other letters, it usually stands for the sound at the beginning of *cow*. Write the word that names each picture.

cents	center	cereal	computer
camera	corn	cabin	cymbal
celery	camel	comb	ceiling

1. cereal
2. cabin
3. center
4. computer
5. corn
6. camera
7. cymbal
8. cents
9. ceiling
10. comb
11. camel
12. celery

Page 203 — Initial Soft c

Name _____

Circle the soft *c* word that best finishes each sentence. Write it on the line.

1. Centerville will __celebrate__ its centennial. — (celebrate), enjoying, calling
2. This means that the __city__ is 100 years old. — candy, town, (city)
3. Centerville is __certain__ to have a big party. — contain, (certain), sure
4. The __citizens__ will get together. — people, cousins, (citizens)
5. They will come to the __center__ of town. — (center), candle, middle
6. A __celebrity__ will make a speech. — calendar, (celebrity), star

Page 204 — Initial Hard c

Name _____

Write the hard *c* words to complete the rhyme.

| cackle | cat | cocoon | cold |
| colt | couch | cover | cow |

When the leaves turn gold, And the days grow __cold__,

When wood fires crackle, And starlings __cackle__,

Animals may discover It is time to take __cover__.

Caterpillar will sleep soon In its warm __cocoon__.

Mouse will say, "Ouch!" And hide under the __couch__.

"To the barn I must bolt," Says the frisky __colt__.

"Where is my green grass now?" Complains the __cow__.

"I will lie here and grow fat," Purrs the warm, cozy __cat__.

Write the answers to the questions.
Possible responses are shown.

1. What season is the poem about?
   fall or autumn

2. Why do the animals need to take cover?
   because it is getting cold outside

Page 205 — Initial Hard and Soft c • Reading Words in Context

Name _____

Read the story, and answer the questions.

Cooking Up Trouble

Cindy loves to cook. So does her brother, Carl. One day they got out their old cookbook. They looked at the recipes—Celery Salad, Country Ham, Corn on the Cob, and Candied Yams.

"Ugh!" said Carl. "We have tried every recipe here. This cookbook is boring."

"You are certainly right!" answered Cindy. "I have an idea. We can make something new. We can make up our own cookbook."

So they did. Here is the table of contents for their new cookbook:

| Cucumber Candy . . . .1 | Cement Cookies . . . . .5 |
| Centipede Stew . . . . .2 | Cedar Cereal . . . . . . .6 |

1. What recipes were in the old cookbook?
   Celery Salad, Country Ham, Corn on the Cob, Candied Yams

2. Why did the children make a new cookbook?
   Their old cookbook was boring. They had already tried every recipe in it.

3. Which of the new recipes would you be willing to try?
   Responses will vary.

54

Phonics Practice Book Teacher's Edition

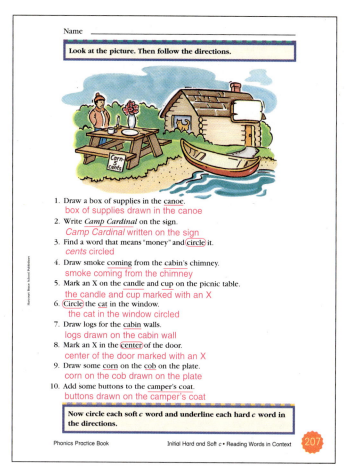

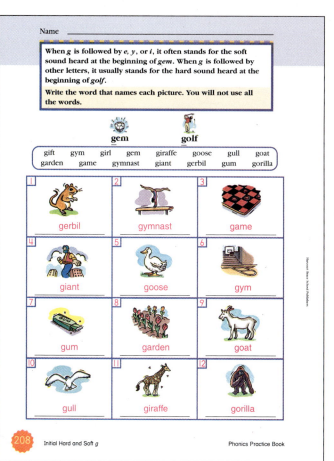

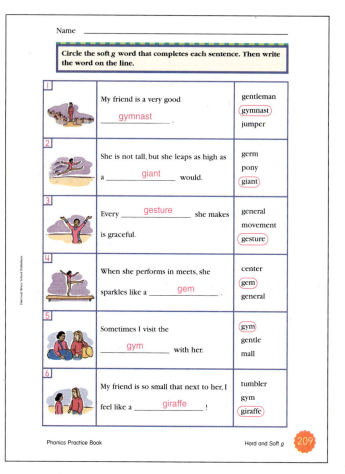

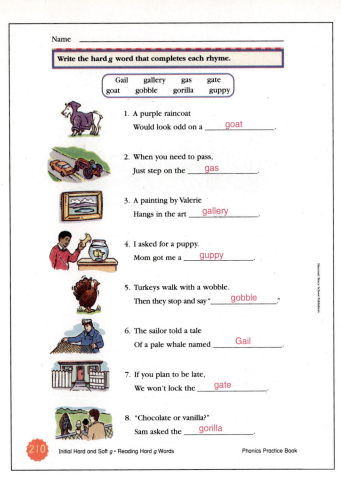

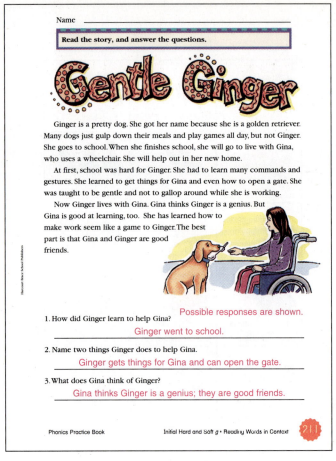

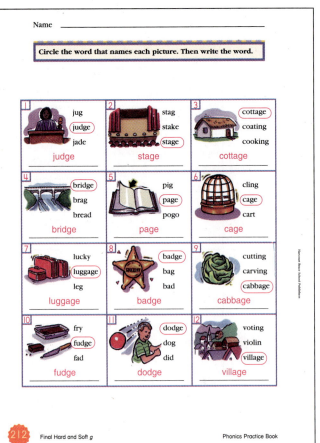

56

Page 214

Name _____

REVIEW — Find the words that fit the clues. Write the words in the puzzle.

giggle center citrus cage gas giraffe
page giant fence edge goat icy go

ACROSS
1. The middle part
2. Laugh
6. Huge
7. A part of a book
9. Something that divides two back yards
10. Fuel for a car

DOWN
1. Safe home for some kinds of pets
2. An animal with a very long neck
3. The rim
4. An animal with a beard
5. A kind of fruit
8. Frozen
10. The opposite of *stop*

Crossword answers:
1 across: center
2 across: giggle
6 across: giant
7 across: page
9 across: fence
10 across: gas
1 down: cage
2 down: giraffe
3 down: edge
4 down: goat
5 down: citrus
8 down: icy

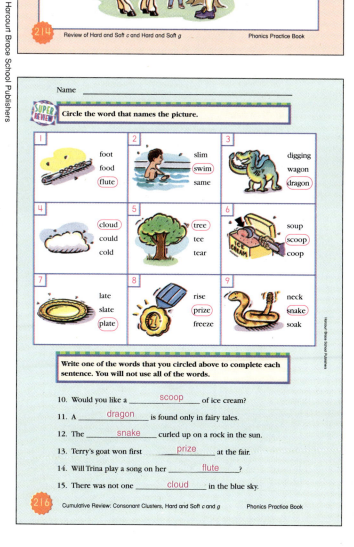

Review of Hard and Soft *c* and Hard and Soft *g* — Phonics Practice Book — 214

Page 215

Name _____

REVIEW — Circle the word that answers each riddle. Then write the word.

1. We are tiny rodents that scurry and squeak. We are __**mice**__.
    make (mice) mug

2. I do not like to brag, but I am very, very smart. I am a __**genius**__.
    (genius) canes gentle

3. I am a bed, but I do not have pillows or blankets. I am a home for flowers. I am a __**garden**__.
    carton gerbil (garden)

4. I am not a boy. I am a __**girl**__.
    grill curl (girl)

5. I say "honk, honk," but I do not have a horn. I am a __**goose**__.
    (goose) cost gas

6. I am shaped like a star. A sheriff may wear me. I am a __**badge**__.
    back (badge) beg

7. I seem very big to you. To me, you look small. I am a __**giant**__.
    game (giant) icing

8. I work in a courtroom. I decide who is right and who is wrong. I am a __**judge**__.
    jug goat (judge)

9. I am a small wooden bird. I live in a clock. I am a __**cuckoo**__.
    pogo (cuckoo) kicker

10. My name sounds like a country for automobiles. But I am really a flower. I am a __**carnation**__.
    garden certain (carnation)

Review: Hard and Soft *c* and Hard and Soft *g* — 215

Page 216

Name _____

SUPER REVIEW — Circle the word that names the picture.

1. foot / food / (flute)
2. slim / (swim) / same
3. digging / wagon / (dragon)
4. (cloud) / could / cold
5. (tree) / tee / tear
6. soup / (scoop) / coop
7. late / slate / (plate)
8. rise / (prize) / freeze
9. neck / (snake) / soak

Write one of the words that you circled above to complete each sentence. You will not use all of the words.

10. Would you like a __**scoop**__ of ice cream?
11. A __**dragon**__ is found only in fairy tales.
12. The __**snake**__ curled up on a rock in the sun.
13. Terry's goat won first __**prize**__ at the fair.
14. Will Trina play a song on her __**flute**__?
15. There was not one __**cloud**__ in the blue sky.

Cumulative Review: Consonant Clusters, Hard and Soft *c* and *g* — Phonics Practice Book — 216

Page 217

Name _____

SUPER REVIEW — Write each word under the correct heading.

adult cow girl skunk twins camp crab
giraffe squid village child fly judge
street wasp city garden pond student

People	Places	Animals
adult	camp	giraffe
child	city	cow
girl	garden	crab
judge	pond	fly
student	street	skunk
twins	village	squid
		wasp

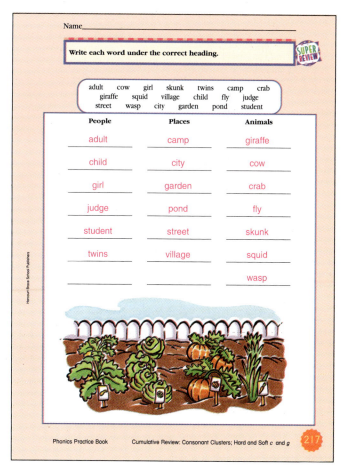

Cumulative Review: Consonant Clusters; Hard and Soft *c* and *g* — 217

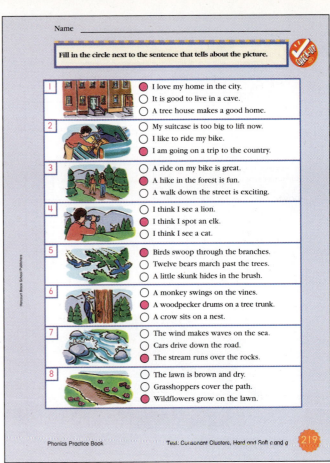
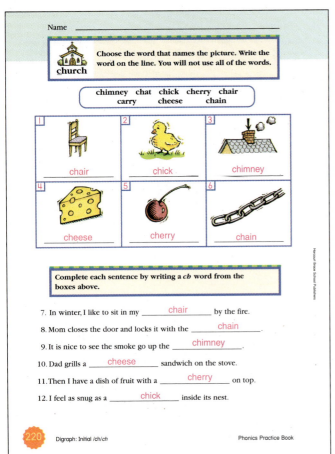

58

Phonics Practice Book Teacher's Edition

Page 222

Name _____

🖌 brush — Write the word from the box that answers each clue.

sheep	shell	cash	shop	shrimp
dish	shut	hush	ship	shrink

1. It begins like *shark* and rhymes with *deep*. It is a kind of animal. What is it? **sheep**
2. It begins like *cab* and rhymes with *mash*. When you have it, you can save it or spend it. What is it? **cash**
3. It begins like *bum* and rhymes with *brush*. You say it to stop a noise. What is it? **hush**
4. It begins like *shrub* and rhymes with *drink*. It happens when something gets smaller. What is it? **shrink**
5. It begins like *shark* and rhymes with *stop*. You do it in a store. What is it? **shop**
6. It begins like *shark* and rhymes with *well*. You might find one by the sea. What is it? **shell**
7. It begins like *shark* and ends like *zip*. It is something that floats in the sea. What is it? **ship**
8. It begins like *did* and rhymes with *fish*. It is another word for *plate*. What is it? **dish**
9. It begins like *shark* and rhymes with *cut*. You do it to a door to close it. What is it? **shut**
10. It begins like *shrub* and rhymes with *blimp*. It is a small sea animal. What is it? **shrimp**

Digraphs: Initial and Final /sh/*sh*; Initial /shr/*shr*

Page 223

Name _____

Choose the word that fits each clue. Write the words in the puzzle.

rush	shrink	brush	shore	sheep
fish	shark	shake	shrub	shorts

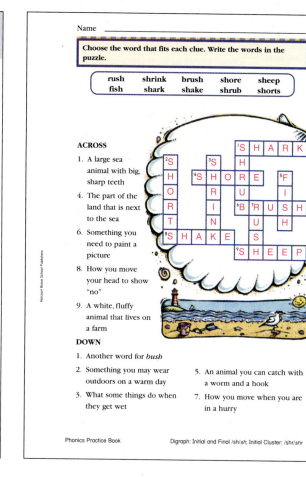

ACROSS
1. A large sea animal with big, sharp teeth
4. The part of the land that is next to the sea
6. Something you need to paint a picture
8. How you move your head to show "no"
9. A white, fluffy animal that lives on a farm

DOWN
1. Another word for *bush*
2. Something you may wear outdoors on a warm day
3. What some things do when they get wet
5. An animal you can catch with a worm and a hook
7. How you move when you are in a hurry

Digraph: Initial and Final /sh/*sh*; Initial Cluster: /shr/*shr*

Page 224

Name _____

thumb tooth three

Write the word that names each picture. You will not use all of the words.

thermos	path	three	throne	thorn	thirteen	moth	mouth
bath	tooth	thimble	throat	think	thief	thread	thirty

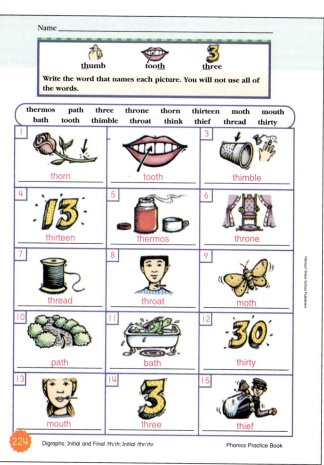

1. thorn
2. tooth
3. thimble
4. thirteen
5. thermos
6. throne
7. thread
8. throat
9. moth
10. path
11. bath
12. thirty
13. mouth
14. three
15. thief

Digraphs: Initial and Final /th/*th*; Initial /thr/*thr*

Page 225

Name _____

Read the page from Michael's diary. Then use a *th* or *thr* word from the diary to complete each sentence below.

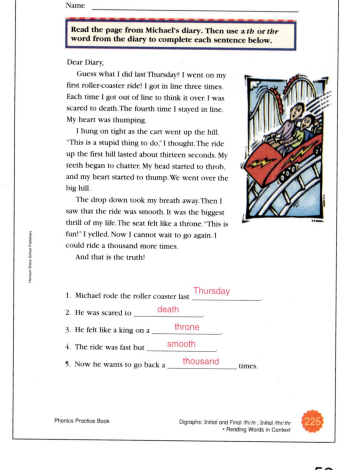

Dear Diary,
 Guess what I did last Thursday? I went on my first roller-coaster ride! I got in line three times. Each time I got out of line to think it over. I was scared to death. The fourth time I stayed in line. My heart was thumping.
 I hung on tight as the cart went up the hill. "This is a stupid thing to do," I thought. The ride up the first hill lasted about thirteen seconds. My teeth began to chatter. My head started to throb, and my heart started to thump. We went over the big hill.
 The drop down took my breath away. Then I saw that the ride was smooth. It was the biggest thrill of my life. The seat felt like a throne. "This is fun!" I yelled. Now I cannot wait to go again. I could ride a thousand more times.
 And that is the truth!

1. Michael rode the roller coaster last **Thursday**.
2. He was scared to **death**.
3. He felt like a king on a **throne**.
4. The ride was fast but **smooth**.
5. Now he wants to go back a **thousand** times.

Digraphs: Initial and Final /th/*th*; Initial /thr/*thr*
• Reading Words in Context

Phonics Practice Book Teacher's Edition   59

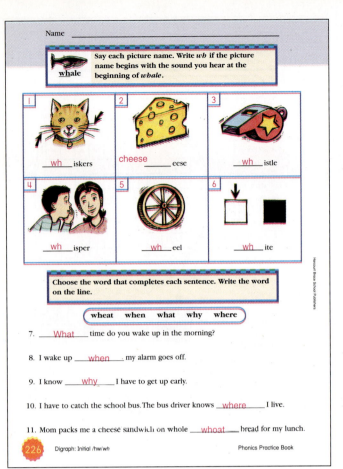
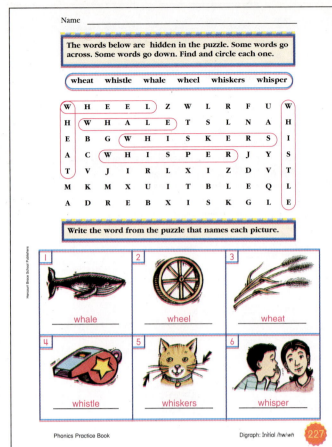
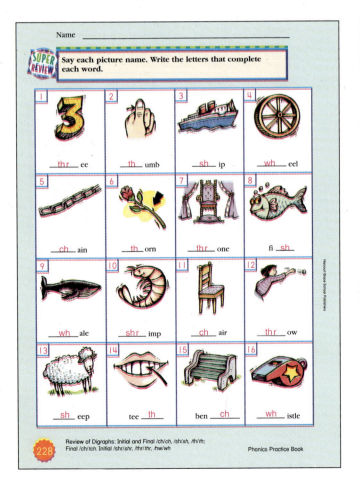
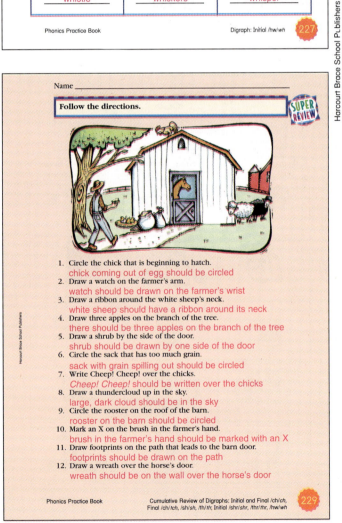

Name _____

phone
graph

Choose the word that answers each riddle. Write the word on the line.

1. I start out in a camera. I end up in an album. I am a ___photo___.
   photo   pay   phrase

2. I am a chart that shows numbers. I may have lines or bars. I am a ___graph___.
   graph   great   grill

3. I am more than a word. I am less than a sentence. I am a ___phrase___.
   phrase   phone   prize

4. I am a name written down. If you meet a sports star, you might ask for one. I am an ___autograph___.
   enough   autograph   around

5. I am a large bird. I have a long, pretty tail. I am a ___pheasant___.
   peanut   pheasant   photo

6. I am something you talk into. I am a ___phone___.
   phone   picnic   pink

7. I am a group of sentences. I am a ___paragraph___.
   graph   paragraph   pillow

8. I am a store where people can buy medicine. I am a ___pharmacy___.
   pharmacy   farm   phone

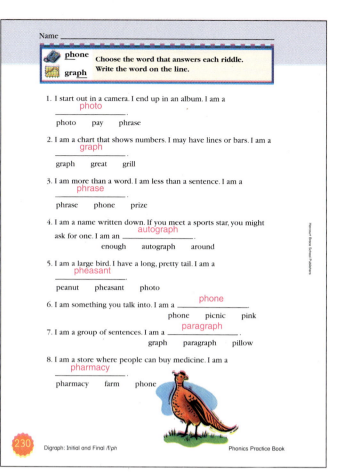

230 Digraph: Initial and Final /f/ph   Phonics Practice Book

Name _____

laugh

Listen to the sound the letters *gh* stand for in *laugh*. Fill in the circle next to the sentence that tells about the picture.

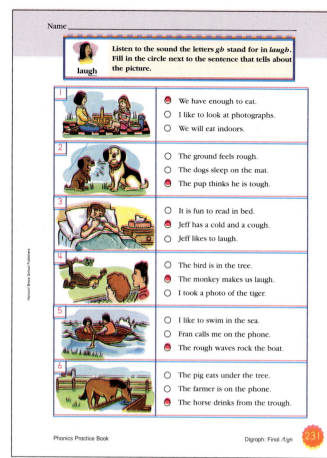

1. ● We have enough to eat.
   ○ I like to look at photographs.
   ○ We will eat indoors.

2. ○ The ground feels rough.
   ○ The dogs sleep on the mat.
   ● The pup thinks he is tough.

3. ○ It is fun to read in bed.
   ● Jeff has a cold and a cough.
   ○ Jeff likes to laugh.

4. ○ The bird is in the tree.
   ● The monkey makes us laugh.
   ○ I took a photo of the tiger.

5. ○ I like to swim in the sea.
   ○ Fran calls me on the phone.
   ● The rough waves rock the boat.

6. ○ The pig eats under the tree.
   ○ The farmer is on the phone.
   ● The horse drinks from the trough.

Phonics Practice Book   Digraph: Final /f/gh 231

Name _____

write

Listen to the sound the letters *wr* stand for in *write*. Circle the word that names the picture. Then write the word.

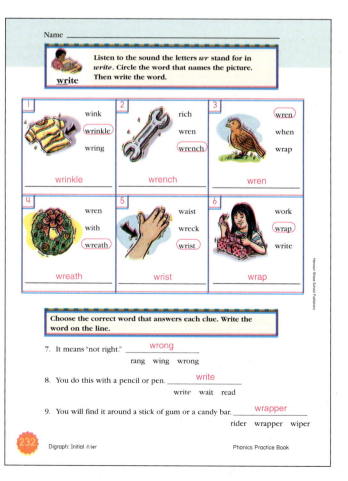

1. wink / (wrinkle) / wring — **wrinkle**
2. rich / wren / (wrench) — **wrench**
3. (wren) / when / wrap — **wren**
4. wren / with / (wreath) — **wreath**
5. waist / wreck / (wrist) — **wrist**
6. work / (wrap) / write — **wrap**

Choose the correct word that answers each clue. Write the word on the line.

7. It means "not right." **wrong**
   rang   wing   wrong

8. You do this with a pencil or pen. **write**
   write   wait   read

9. You will find it around a stick of gum or a candy bar. **wrapper**
   rider   wrapper   wiper

232 Digraph: Initial /r/wr   Phonics Practice Book

Name _____

knight
gnat

Listen to the sound the letters *kn* and *gn* stand for in *knight* and *gnat*. Complete each sentence.

1. I heard a loud ___knock___ on the door.
   cook / knock / night

2. The ___knob___ turned slowly.
   not / cob / knob

3. A little green ___gnome___ stood in the doorway.
   gnome / gum / name

4. He only came up to my ___knee___.
   new / key / knee

5. Please give me a bone to ___gnaw___ on," he said.
   grow / gnaw / gown

6. "I ___know___ you can find one for me," he said.
   know / cow / nail

7. "If you do, I will ___knit___ you a cap."
   knit / kit / nice

8. As he rode away on a giant ___gnat___, I woke up.
   go / gnat / knot

9. Then I ___knew___ it was only a dream.
   not / kit / knew

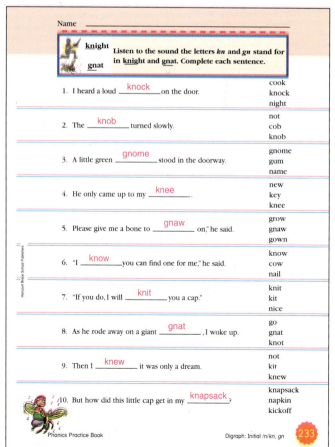

10. But how did this little cap get in my ___knapsack___?
    knapsack / napkin / kickoff

Phonics Practice Book   Digraph: Initial /n/kn, gn 233

Phonics Practice Book Teacher's Edition   61

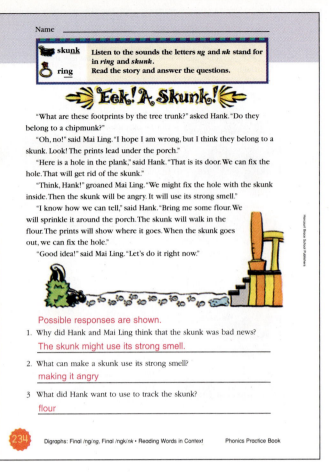
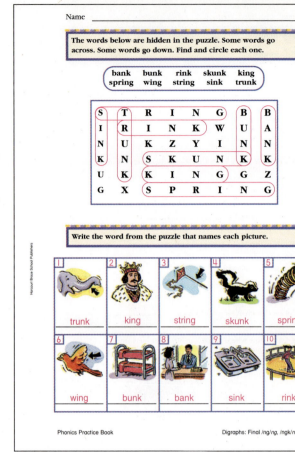

Phonics Practice Book Teacher's Edition

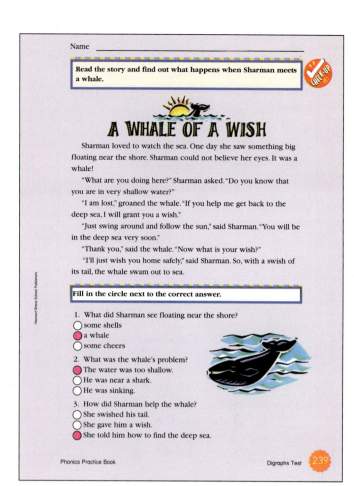
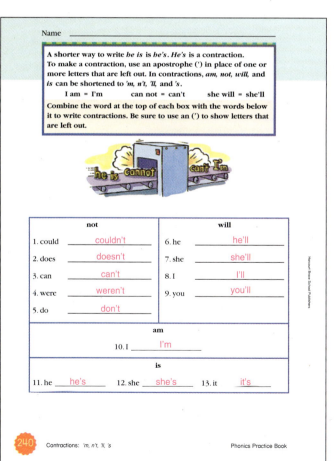
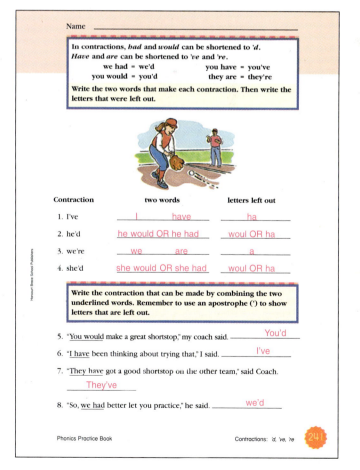

Name _____

REVIEW

For each sentence, form a contraction from the words in parentheses ( ). Write the contraction.

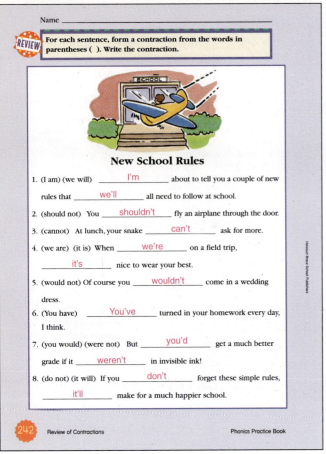

New School Rules

1. (I am) (we will) __I'm__ about to tell you a couple of new rules that __we'll__ all need to follow at school.
2. (should not) You __shouldn't__ fly an airplane through the door.
3. (cannot) At lunch, your snake __can't__ ask for more.
4. (we are) (it is) When __we're__ on a field trip, __it's__ nice to wear your best.
5. (would not) Of course you __wouldn't__ come in a wedding dress.
6. (You have) __You've__ turned in your homework every day, I think.
7. (you would) (were not) But __you'd__ get a much better grade if it __weren't__ in invisible ink!
8. (do not) (it will) If you __don't__ forget these simple rules, __it'll__ make for a much happier school.

242 Review of Contractions   Phonics Practice Book

Name _____

REVIEW

Read the selection. Then answer the questions.

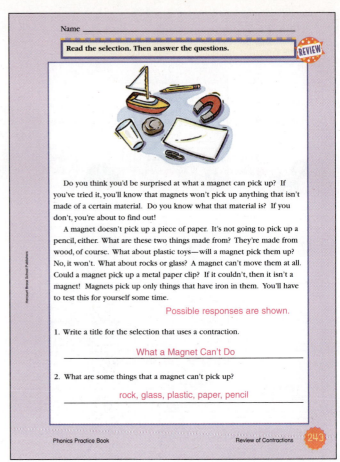

Do you think you'd be surprised at what a magnet can pick up? If you've tried it, you'll know that magnets won't pick up anything that isn't made of a certain material. Do you know what that material is? If you don't, you're about to find out!

A magnet doesn't pick up a piece of paper. It's not going to pick up a pencil, either. What are these two things made from? They're made from wood, of course. What about plastic toys—will a magnet pick them up? No, it won't. What about rocks or glass? A magnet can't move them at all. Could a magnet pick up a metal paper clip? If it couldn't, then it isn't a magnet! Magnets pick up only things that have iron in them. You'll have to test this for yourself some time.

Possible responses are shown.

1. Write a title for the selection that uses a contraction.
   __What a Magnet Can't Do__

2. What are some things that a magnet can't pick up?
   __rock, glass, plastic, paper, pencil__

Phonics Practice Book   Review of Contractions 243

Name _____

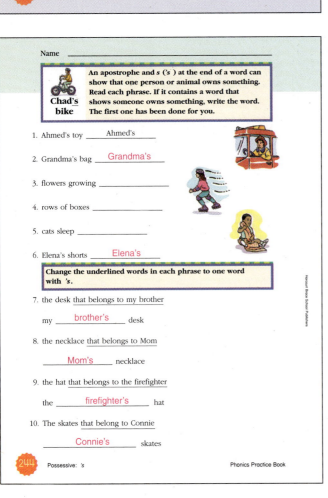

Chad's bike — An apostrophe and s ('s) at the end of a word can show that one person or animal owns something. Read each phrase. If it contains a word that shows someone owns something, write the word. The first one has been done for you.

1. Ahmed's toy __Ahmed's__
2. Grandma's bag __Grandma's__
3. flowers growing _____
4. rows of boxes _____
5. cats sleep _____
6. Elena's shorts __Elena's__

Change the underlined words in each phrase to one word with 's.

7. the desk that belongs to my brother
   my __brother's__ desk
8. the necklace that belongs to Mom
   __Mom's__ necklace
9. the hat that belongs to the firefighter
   the __firefighter's__ hat
10. The skates that belong to Connie
    __Connie's__ skates

244 Possessive: 's   Phonics Practice Book

Name _____

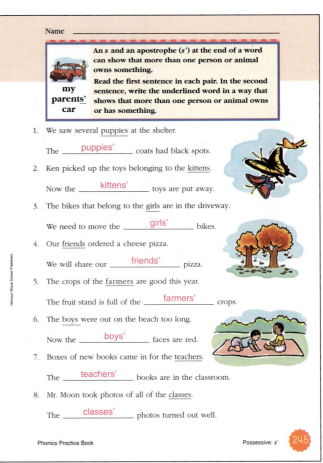

my parents' car — An s and an apostrophe (s') at the end of a word can show that more than one person or animal owns something. Read the first sentence in each pair. In the second sentence, write the underlined word in a way that shows that more than one person or animal owns or has something.

1. We saw several puppies at the shelter.
   The __puppies'__ coats had black spots.
2. Ken picked up the toys belonging to the kittens.
   Now the __kittens'__ toys are put away.
3. The bikes that belong to the girls are in the driveway.
   We need to move the __girls'__ bikes.
4. Our friends ordered a cheese pizza.
   We will share our __friends'__ pizza.
5. The crops of the farmers are good this year.
   The fruit stand is full of the __farmers'__ crops.
6. The boys were out on the beach too long.
   Now the __boys'__ faces are red.
7. Boxes of new books came in for the teachers.
   The __teachers'__ books are in the classroom.
8. Mr. Moon took photos of all of the classes.
   The __classes'__ photos turned out well.

Phonics Practice Book   Possessive: s' 245

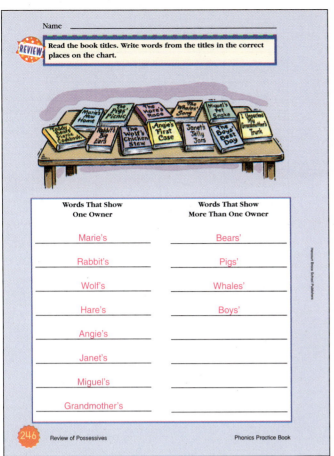

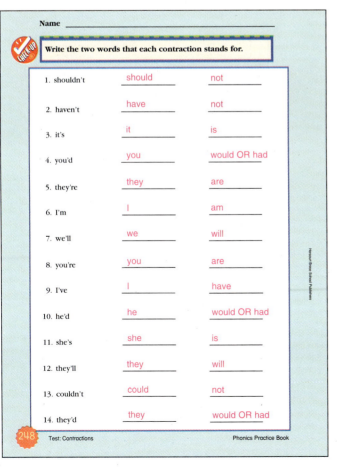

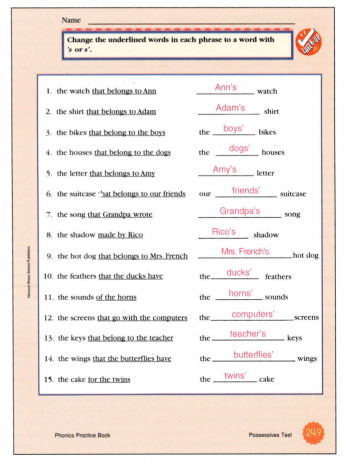

Page 250

Complete each sentence by adding *s*, *es*, *ed*, or *ing* to the word in front of the sentence

Today
I jump.
The frog jumps too.
The frog and I are jumping.
My dad watches us.
Yesterday
The frog jumped, and I did not.

1. play — The Lan family enjoys __playing__ music every day.
2. start — The children __started__ playing when they were very young.
3. sing — Mei Ling __sings__ and plays the flute.
4. want — Tran plays the violin, but last year he __wanted__ to learn to play the harp.
5. wish — He __wishes__ he could play both.
6. listen — Mrs. Lan smiles as she __listens__ to her children play.
7. talk — Last week, they __talked__ about giving a concert.
8. look — They are __looking__ for a place to hold a concert.
9. ask — Last Tuesday, the Lans __asked__ me to help them find a place.
10. wait — The Lans are just __waiting__ for the special day when they can give the concert.

Page 251

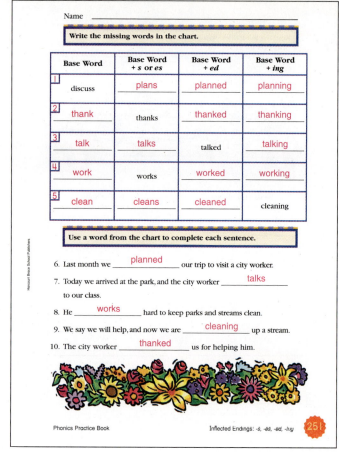

Write the missing words in the chart.

Base Word	Base Word + *s* or *es*	Base Word + *ed*	Base Word + *ing*
1. discuss	plans	planned	planning
2. thank	thanks	thanked	thanking
3. talk	talks	talked	talking
4. work	works	worked	working
5. clean	cleans	cleaned	cleaning

Use a word from the chart to complete each sentence.

6. Last month we __planned__ our trip to visit a city worker.
7. Today we arrived at the park, and the city worker __talks__ to our class.
8. He __works__ hard to keep parks and streams clean.
9. We say we will help, and now we are __cleaning__ up a stream.
10. The city worker __thanked__ us for helping him.

Page 252

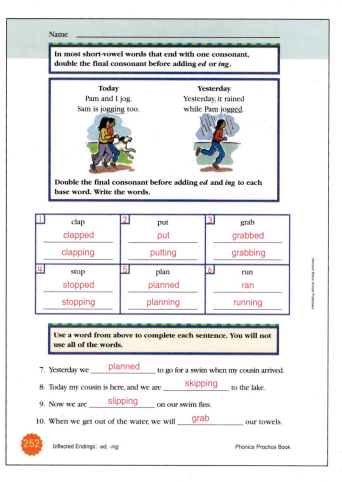

In most short-vowel words that end with one consonant, double the final consonant before adding *ed* or *ing*.

Today
Pam and I jog.
Sam is jogging too.

Yesterday
Yesterday, it rained while Pam jogged.

Double the final consonant before adding *ed* and *ing* to each base word. Write the words.

1. clap	2. put	3. grab
clapped	put	grabbed
clapping	putting	grabbing

4. stop	5. plan	6. run
stopped	planned	ran
stopping	planning	running

Use a word from above to complete each sentence. You will not use all of the words.

7. Yesterday we __planned__ to go for a swim when my cousin arrived.
8. Today my cousin is here, and we are __skipping__ to the lake.
9. Now we are __slipping__ on our swim fins.
10. When we get out of the water, we will __grab__ our towels.

Page 253

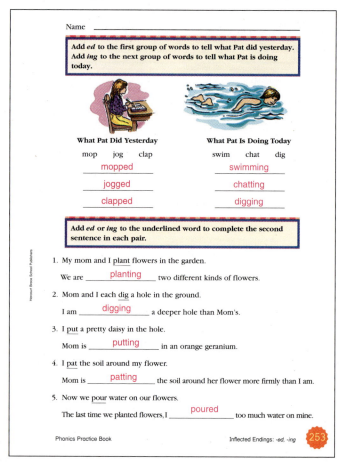

Add *ed* to the first group of words to tell what Pat did yesterday. Add *ing* to the next group of words to tell what Pat is doing today.

What Pat Did Yesterday
mop jog clap
mopped
jogged
clapped

What Pat Is Doing Today
swim chat dig
swimming
chatting
digging

Add *ed* or *ing* to the underlined word to complete the second sentence in each pair.

1. My mom and I plant flowers in the garden.
   We are __planting__ two different kinds of flowers.
2. Mom and I each dig a hole in the ground.
   I am __digging__ a deeper hole than Mom's.
3. I put a pretty daisy in the hole.
   Mom is __putting__ in an orange geranium.
4. I pat the soil around my flower.
   Mom is __patting__ the soil around her flower more firmly than I am.
5. Now we pour water on our flowers.
   The last time we planted flowers, I __poured__ too much water on mine.

Name _____

REVIEW Read the paragraphs, and think about what they tell you.

An Eclipse of the Sun

Have you ever seen an eclipse of the sun? Bet you were wondering what was happening. If so, you saw the sky get dark in the middle of the day.

People long ago were afraid when there was an eclipse. They would start running and screaming. But we know now that an eclipse is nothing to be afraid of.

An eclipse happens when the moon passes in a straight line between the earth and the sun. For a short time, the moon blocks the light of the sun. Then the moon passes out of the way, and sunlight once again touches the earth.

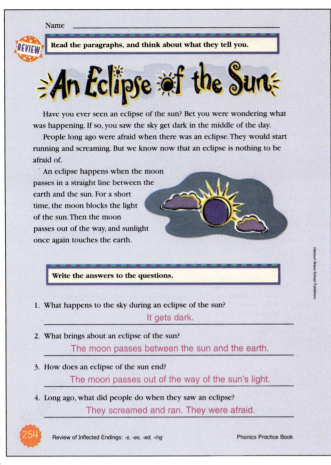

Write the answers to the questions.

1. What happens to the sky during an eclipse of the sun?
   It gets dark.
2. What brings about an eclipse of the sun?
   The moon passes between the sun and the earth.
3. How does an eclipse of the sun end?
   The moon passes out of the way of the sun's light.
4. Long ago, what did people do when they saw an eclipse?
   They screamed and ran. They were afraid.

254   Review of Inflected Endings: -s, -es, -ed, -ing

Name _____

REVIEW Add the correct ending to the underlined base word in each sentence. Write the new words in the puzzle.

Across
1. My canary <u>sing</u> as I eat my breakfast.
3. The girl is <u>bring</u> some food for her pet.
5. My cat <u>rub</u> against my legs last night.
7. The rabbit <u>munch</u> on the carrots I give it.
9. My cat <u>purr</u> when I stroked her fur yesterday.
11. The boy <u>hunt</u> for his lost book last week.
13. I am <u>run</u> in a race today.

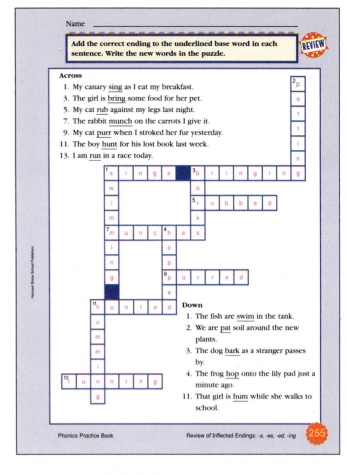

Down
1. The fish are <u>swim</u> in the tank.
2. We are <u>pat</u> soil around the new plants.
3. The dog <u>bark</u> as a stranger passes by.
4. The frog <u>hop</u> onto the lily pad just a minute ago.
11. That girl is <u>hum</u> while she walks to school.

255   Review of Inflected Endings: -s, -es, -ed, -ing

Name _____

In words that end with silent *e*, drop the *e* before adding *ed* or *ing*. Drop the silent *e* and add *ed* and *ing* to each base word. Write the new words.

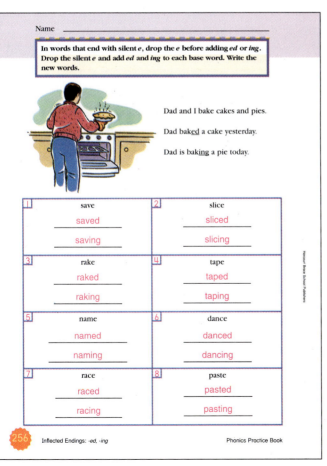

Dad and I bake cakes and pies.
Dad bak<u>ed</u> a cake yesterday.
Dad is bak<u>ing</u> a pie today.

1	save	2	slice
	saved		sliced
	saving		slicing
3	rake	4	tape
	raked		taped
	raking		taping
5	name	6	dance
	named		danced
	naming		dancing
7	race	8	paste
	raced		pasted
	racing		pasting

256   Inflected Endings: -ed, -ing

Name _____

Read the story and answer the questions.

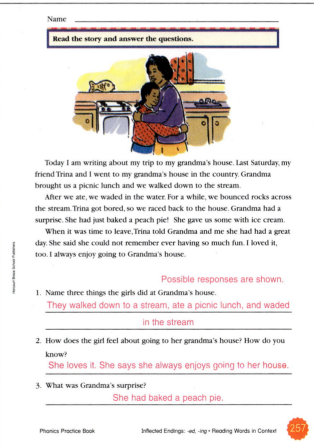

Today I am writing about my trip to my grandma's house. Last Saturday, my friend Trina and I went to my grandma's house in the country. Grandma brought us a picnic lunch and we walked down to the stream.

After we ate, we waded in the water. For a while, we bounced rocks across the stream. Trina got bored, so we raced back to the house. Grandma had a surprise. She had just baked a peach pie! She gave us some with ice cream.

When it was time to leave, Trina told Grandma and me she had had a great day. She said she could not remember ever having so much fun. I loved it, too. I always enjoy going to Grandma's house.

Possible responses are shown.

1. Name three things the girls did at Grandma's house.
   They walked down to a stream, ate a picnic lunch, and waded in the stream
2. How does the girl feel about going to her grandma's house? How do you know?
   She loves it. She says she always enjoys going to her house.
3. What was Grandma's surprise?
   She had baked a peach pie.

257   Inflected Endings: -ed, -ing • Reading Words in Context

---

Phonics Practice Book Teacher's Edition   67

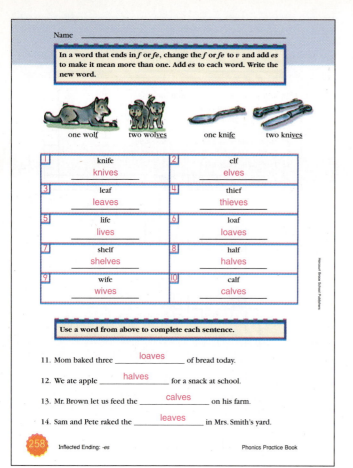
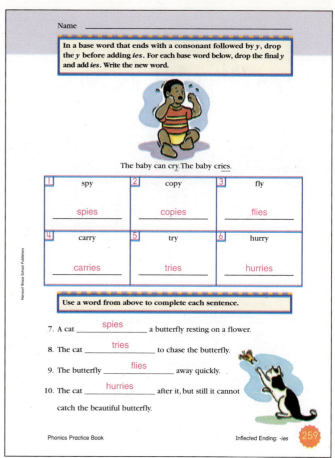
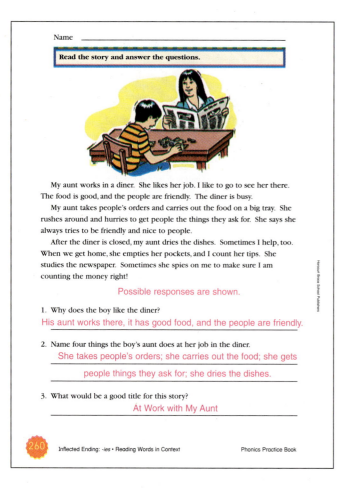
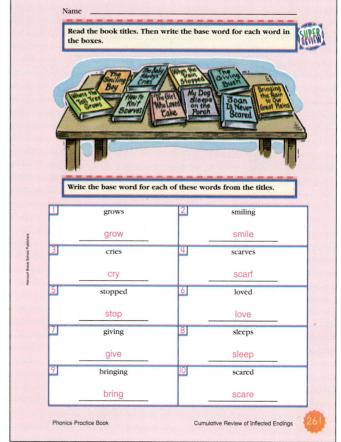

Name _____

Write the base word for the underlined word in each sentence.

1. Our dad <u>tries</u> to teach us to do things to help clean up the earth. __try__
2. He <u>likes</u> for us to recycle paper and cans each week. __like__
3. He also <u>wants</u> us to grow some of our own food. __want__
4. My little sister and I <u>planted</u> some bean seeds in pots. __plant__
5. Dad said, "Put them in the window and make sure the sun is <u>shining</u> on them." __shine__
6. Every day my sister <u>rushes</u> over to look at the pots. __rush__
7. Earlier this morning she shouted, "They <u>sprouted</u> last night!" __sprout__
8. My little sister <u>clapped</u> her hands when she saw the tiny plants. __clap__
9. I saw little green shoots <u>popping</u> up through the soil. __pop__
10. Soon we will be <u>eating</u> the beans that we have grown. __eat__
11. My dad has <u>asked</u> us to think of some other ways we can keep the earth clean. __ask__
12. He says our <u>lives</u> will be better if the earth is clean and healthy. __life__

262 Cumulative Review of Inflected Endings

Name _____

Write the base word for the underlined word in each sentence.

1. Last week we <u>planned</u> a camping trip. __plan__
2. Today we are <u>staying</u> in a tent at our beautiful campsite. __stay__
3. The sun is <u>shining</u> brightly. __shine__
4. But every time we leave the campsite, a bear <u>tries</u> to get our food. __try__
5. Mom <u>fusses</u> at us if we leave food sitting out. __fuss__
6. We are <u>hoping</u> the bear has gotten tired of our campsite, but it hasn't. __hope__
7. It keeps <u>walking</u> up to our campsite when we are not there. __walk__
8. A little while ago, we tried to go back to the tent but we <u>stopped</u> when we saw the bear. __stop__
9. It was eating all of our <u>loaves</u> of honey bread. __loaf__
10. Dad <u>wants</u> to scare the bear away. __want__
11. We are <u>getting</u> tired of waiting. __get__
12. Finally the bear <u>runs</u> away! __run__

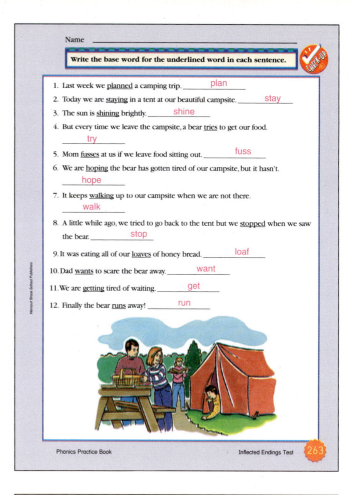

Inflected Endings Test 263

Name _____

Complete the chart by adding the ending at the top to the base word.

		s or es	ing	ed
1	start	starts	starting	started
2	skid	skids	skidding	skidded
3	wish	wishes	wishing	wished
4	play	plays	playing	played
5	watch	watches	watching	watched
6	clap	claps	clapping	clapped

Write the base word.

7	grabbed — grab	8	sings — sing	9	trying — try
10	dishes — dish	11	leaves — leaf	12	stopping — stop
13	spies — spy	14	picked — pick	15	chatting — chat
16	pitches — pitch	17	dries — dry	18	taped — tape

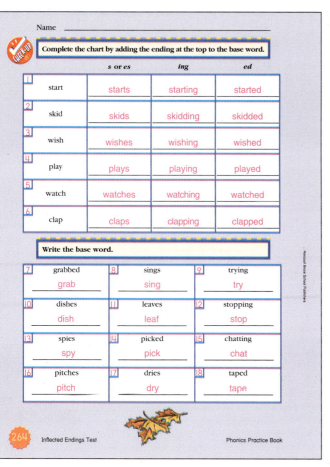

264 Inflected Endings Test

Name _____

A prefix is added to the beginning of a base word to make a new word with a different meaning. Write the word with un- or re- that matches each meaning.

un = not
re = again

1	use again — reuse	2	not kind — unkind	3	join again — rejoin
4	build again — rebuild	5	not able — unable	6	write again — rewrite
7	not true — untrue	8	not happy — unhappy	9	fill again — refill
10	not afraid — unafraid	11	tell again — retell	12	not safe — unsafe

Add the prefix im- to each word. Then write a word to complete each sentence.

im = not

| 13 | patient — impatient | 14 | perfect — imperfect | 15 | polite — impolite |

16. My family says that being late is __impolite__
17. When we are getting ready to go somewhere, they are quite __impatient__ with me.
18. I think that makes them __imperfect__, too!

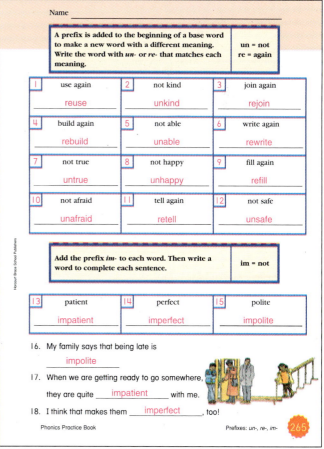

Prefixes: un-, re-, im- 265

Phonics Practice Book Teacher's Edition   69

Name _____

Add the prefix *im-* or *re-* to the underlined word to complete each sentence.

1. If water is not clean and pure, then it is __impure__.
2. If you check your work again, you __recheck__ it.
3. If you pay back money that you owe, you __repay__ it.
4. If you tie your shoe again, you __retie__ it.
5. If an action is not proper, then it is __improper__.
6. If someone is not mature, then he or she is __immature__.
7. If you place an item back on the shelf, you __replace__ it.
8. If something is not possible, then it is __impossible__.
9. If you read a book a second time, you __reread__ it.
10. If you turn in work that is not perfect, it might be called __imperfect__.

Add the prefix *re-* to each base word.

11. pack __repack__
12. cover __recover__
13. load __reload__
14. tie __retie__
15. do __redo__

266 Prefixes: *re-, im-* Phonics Practice Book

Name _____

Read the selection, and then answer the question.

Bats, Bats, Bats

Many stories told about bats are untrue. That is why people may react badly when they see bats. Many things that bats do in stories and movies are impossible. Bats can fly like birds. But unlike birds, bats are mammals. All other mammals are unable to fly.

Many bats live in caves. If you go during the day to see bats fly out of a cave, you may become impatient. Bats sleep all day, hanging upside down. At sunset they unfold their wings. Then they fly out of the cave to rejoin the outside world.

Bats fly around looking for food. They help people by eating insects that are pests. So, the next time you see a bat, don't be afraid. If someone tells you something unlikely about bats, ask the person to recheck their facts.

Possible responses are shown.

1. What can be said of many of the things bats do in stories and movies?
   __They are impossible.__
2. Why do some people react badly when they see bats?
   __They have heard many untrue stories about bats.__
3. How does the selection say bats are different from birds?
   __Bats are mammals.__
4. How do bats spend their time during the day?
   __They sleep all day.__
5. How do bats help people?
   __They eat insects that are pests.__

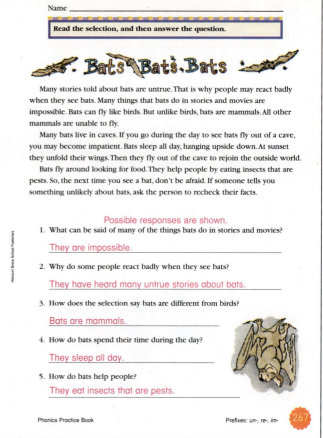

Phonics Practice Book Prefixes: *un-, re-, im-* 267

Name _____

non = not or without   pre = before   dis = the opposite of
Use the prefixes *non*, *pre*, and *dis* to write a word to match each meaning.

1. not a believer	2. to pay before	3. the opposite of *like*
nonbeliever	prepay	dislike
4. not making sense	5. to judge before the right time	6. the opposite of *honest*
nonsense	prejudge	dishonest
7. not toxic	8. to plan before	9. to view before
nontoxic	preplan	preview
10. without a stop	11. the opposite of *appear*	12. the opposite of *order*
nonstop	disappear	disorder

Use a word you just wrote to complete each sentence. You will not use all of the words.

13. The messy room was in a state of __disorder__.
14. Something was sure to get lost and __disappear__.
15. We sat down to __preplan__ who would do the job.
16. Then we worked __nonstop__ to get the work done.

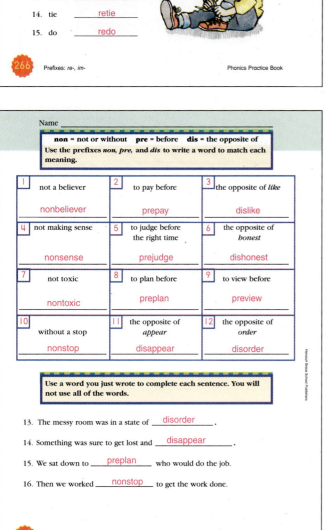

268 Prefixes: *non-, pre-, dis-* Phonics Practice Book

Name _____

Add the prefix *pre-* or *dis-* to the underlined word to complete each sentence.

1. If you do not continue to play a game, you __discontinue__ it.
2. If you are not yet a teen, you are a __preteen__.
3. If you do not feel comfort, then you might feel __discomfort__.
4. The steps a pilot follows before a flight are called __preflight__ checks.
5. Things that happened before historic times are __prehistoric__.
6. A baseball team that does not have the advantage of having good hitters is usually at a __disadvantage__.

Add the prefix *non-* to each base word.

7. verbal __nonverbal__   8. skid __nonskid__
9. sense __nonsense__   10. stop __nonstop__

Write a word you just wrote to complete each sentence.

11. Mom says that buying fancy tennis shoes is __nonsense__.
12. I think good shoes are important when you play sports __nonstop__.
13. I even told her that the __nonskid__ soles would keep me from slipping.
14. She did not say anything, but her __nonverbal__ clues still told me "no."

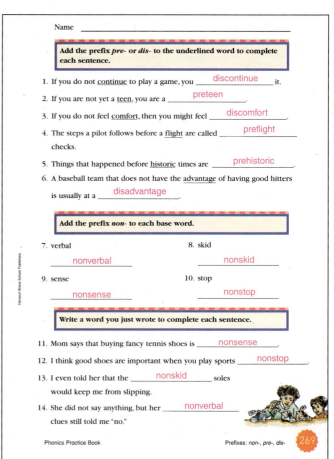

Phonics Practice Book Prefixes: *non-, pre-, dis-* 269

---

70 Phonics Practice Book Teacher's Edition

Name _____

Read the selection, and answer the questions.

What Happened to the Dinosaurs?

Experts disagree about what happened to the creatures that predated other animals. Some scientists say that the dinosaurs disappeared because of changes in the weather. They think it became too cold for dinosaurs to live.

Other scientists say that a huge meteor crashed into the Earth. They think clouds of dust killed many kinds of plants. Many dinosaurs would have had nothing to eat.

Since there are no records of that time, it is hard to disprove one idea or the other. People may wonder for a long time what really happened to those prehistoric creatures. Until proof is found, people can study dinosaurs' nonextinct relatives—reptiles and birds.

Possible responses are shown.

1. Why could a meteor have caused dinosaurs to die out?
   The dust would have destroyed plants, leaving many dinosaurs with nothing to eat.

2. Why is it hard to disprove ideas about dinosaurs?
   There are no records of that time.

3. What nonextinct relatives of dinosaurs can we study today?
   reptiles and birds

270 Prefixes: non-, pre-, dis- • Reading Words in Context — Phonics Practice Book

---

Name _____

The words below are in the puzzle. Some words go down. Some words go across. Find and circle each one.

| prejudge | disband | improper | undo | nonstick | pretest |
| untrue | refill | nonsense | disobey | impolite | reheat |

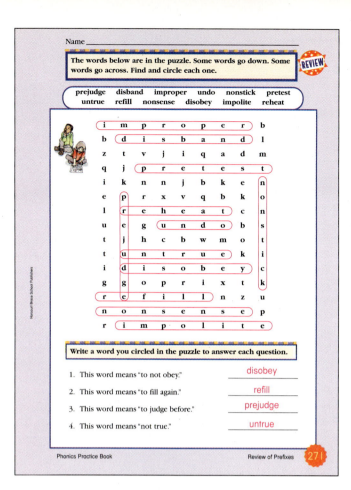

Write a word you circled in the puzzle to answer each question.

1. This word means "to not obey." *disobey*
2. This word means "to fill again." *refill*
3. This word means "to judge before." *prejudge*
4. This word means "not true." *untrue*

Phonics Practice Book — Review of Prefixes 271

Name _____

 Read the letter, and answer the questions.

Dear Misha,

Did you know that some kinds of wolves are in danger of becoming extinct? Some people in my state are trying to rebuild the wolf population in my area. It is uncertain whether they will be able to help. Some people dislike the idea of having wolves rejoin the wildlife here. They feel it will be unsafe for farm animals. But I think that's nonsense. If the wolves don't get help, it will be impossible for them to recover and live in the wild. What do you think? I'd like to hear whether you agree or disagree with me.

Your pen pal,
Josh

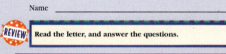

Possible responses are shown.

1. Why did Josh write to Misha?
   to tell him about wolves in danger

2. Why is Josh not sure if the group will be able to help the wolves?
   Some people are upset by the group's efforts.

3. Why do some people dislike the idea of the wolves rejoining the local wildlife?
   They think wolves will harm farm animals.

4. What does Josh think about wolves?
   He likes them. He wants to help them.

272 Review of Prefixes • Reading Words in Context — Phonics Practice Book

---

Name _____

The suffixes -ly and -ful can be added to the end of base words to change their meaning.
-ly = in a certain way
-ful = full of or enough to fill
Add the suffix to each word below it. Write the new words.

-ly
1. slow — *slowly*
2. loud — *loudly*
3. quiet — *quietly*
4. neat — *neatly*
5. quick — *quickly*
6. poor — *poorly*

-ful
7. care — *careful*
8. help — *helpful*
9. thought — *thoughtful*
10. thank — *thankful*
11. cheer — *cheerful*
12. hope — *hopeful*

Use some of the new words you made to complete the sentences.

13. I wanted to finish my homework *quickly* so I could go outside and play.

14. I wrote my spelling words *neatly* so that they were easy to read.

15. I had a question about my math homework, and my sister was *helpful*.

16. I was *thankful* that she could help.

17. I closed my books and *quietly* put my things away.

18. My sister said that I was *thoughtful* for being so quiet.

Phonics Practice Book — Suffixes: -ly, -ful 273

Phonics Practice Book Teacher's Edition — 71

Page 274

Name _____

Add -ly or -ful to each base word to complete each sentence.

1. care — We are always __careful__ when we cross the street.
2. safe — The crossing guard helps us get __safely__ to the other side.
3. brave — She __bravely__ stops traffic for us.
4. near — One day there was __nearly__ an accident.
5. foolish — A little boy __foolishly__ dashed in front of a car.
6. Fortunate — __Fortunately__, the car was able to stop.
7. quick — If the driver had not reacted __quickly__, the boy could have been hurt.
8. fear — The driver was __fearful__ that someone had been hurt.
9. thank — When she saw that no one was hurt, she looked __thankful__.
10. tear — The little boy was fine but __tearful__.
11. help — The crossing guard was __helpful__ in getting the boy to calm down.
12. kind — The guard __kindly__ explained to the boy what he should do next time.

Suffixes: -ly, -ful — 274

Page 275

Name _____

able = able to be, able to give   less = without
Add the suffix -able or -less to write a word to match each definition.

1. able to be washed — washable	2. without joy — joyless	3. able to give comfort — comfortable
4. without sleep — sleepless	5. able to be noticed — noticeable	6. able to be remarked upon — remarkable
7. without a care — careless	8. without thought — thoughtless	9. able to be worked — workable

Add -able or -less to the base word to complete each phrase.

10. port __portable__ television
11. sugar __sugarless__ gum
12. value __valuable__ jewelry (hint: drop the final e)
13. seed __seedless__ grapes
14. adore __adorable__ teddy bear (hint: drop the final e)
15. love __lovable__ pet (hint: drop the final e)

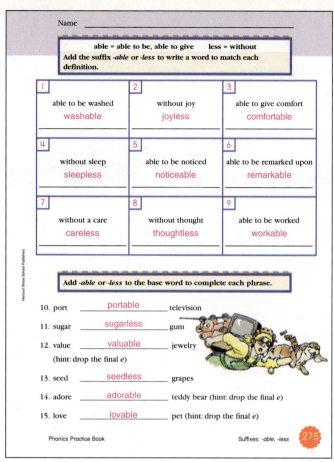

Suffixes: -able, -less — 275

Page 276

Name _____

Choose the word that completes each sentence. Write the words in the puzzle.

toothless   thoughtless   cloudless
washable   remarkable   tasteless
adorable   helpless   portable

Crossword answers:
- 1 across: tasteless
- 3 across: portable
- 5 across: cloudless
- 7 across: toothless
- 2 down: remarkable
- 4 down: washable
- 6 down: helpless
- 10 down: adorable
- 1 down: thoughtless

ACROSS
1. Water has no taste. It is _____.
3. My radio is easy to take with me because it is _____.
5. The sky was clear and _____.
7. The baby had a _____ grin.

DOWN
1. Leaving without saying goodbye was _____.
2. I read the most _____ story.
4. I am glad my new shirt is _____.
6. I try to solve my own problems rather than be _____.
10. The new puppy was _____.

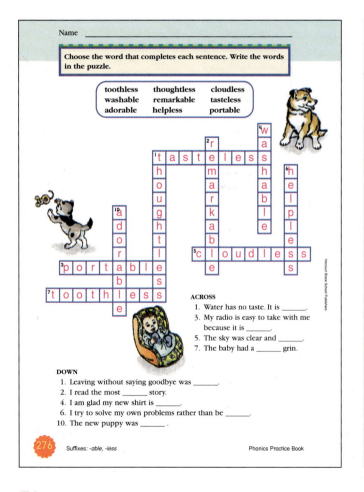

Suffixes: -able, -less — 276

Page 277

Name _____

Add the correct suffix to the underlined word to complete each sentence.

-less   -able
-ly   -ful

1. If the night sky seems to have not even one star, then it is __starless__.
2. If you are moving at a slow speed, you are moving __slowly__.
3. If your jeans can be put in the wash, they are __washable__.
4. If you have enough sugar to fill one cup, you have a __cupful__.
5. If you enjoy the comfort of your bed, it is a __comfortable__ place.
6. If you are full of joy, you are __joyful__.
7. If you did not sleep last night, you had a __sleepless__ night.
8. If you speak in a loud way, your family might say you speak __loudly__.
9. If you had a day full of wonder, you had a __wonderful__ day.
10. If you are brave and without fear, you are a __fearless__ person.
11. If you can train your pet to do tricks, your pet is __trainable__.
12. If you are finishing this page in a quick way, you are finishing __quickly__.

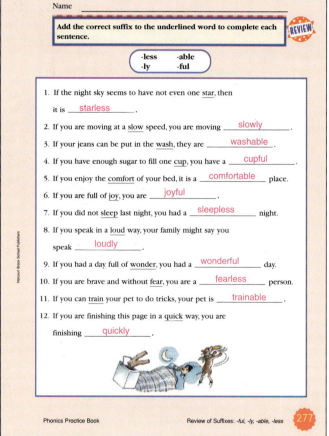

Review of Suffixes: -ful, -ly, -able, -less — 277

Phonics Practice Book Teacher's Edition — 72

Page 278

Name _____

REVIEW — Write a word to complete each sentence.

cupful fearless careful lovely quickly sleepless
neatly remarkable moveable kindly mouthful slowly

1. Please be _careful_ when you hold the new puppy.
2. That animal trick was amazing and _remarkable_.
3. Please write your name _neatly_ on the page.
4. The firefighters were brave and _fearless_ during the blaze.
5. It is impolite to talk with a _mouthful_ of food.
6. My neighbor would like to borrow a _cupful_ of sugar.
7. The police officer spoke _kindly_ to the lost child.
8. This toy has a lot of _moveable_ parts.
9. We spent a _sleepless_ night because the storm was so loud.
10. Mom said the painting I made was _lovely_.
11. The small rabbit ran away _quickly_ when it saw the fox.
12. I chew my food _slowly_ so I can enjoy every bite.

Review of Suffixes — Phonics Practice Book

Page 279

Name _____

SUPER REVIEW — Write the word from the box that fits each meaning.

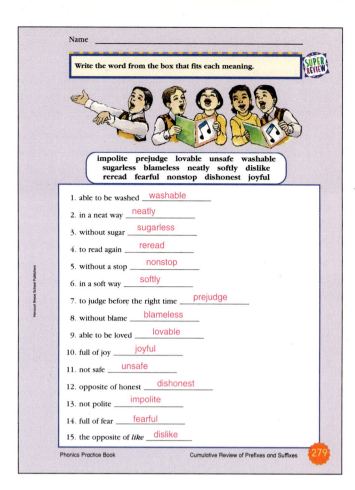

impolite prejudge lovable unsafe washable
sugarless blameless neatly softly dislike
reread fearful nonstop dishonest joyful

1. able to be washed _washable_
2. in a neat way _neatly_
3. without sugar _sugarless_
4. to read again _reread_
5. without a stop _nonstop_
6. in a soft way _softly_
7. to judge before the right time _prejudge_
8. without blame _blameless_
9. able to be loved _lovable_
10. full of joy _joyful_
11. not safe _unsafe_
12. opposite of honest _dishonest_
13. not polite _impolite_
14. full of fear _fearful_
15. the opposite of *like* _dislike_

Phonics Practice Book — Cumulative Review of Prefixes and Suffixes

Page 280

Name _____

SUPER REVIEW — Write the prefix or suffix that completes each statement.

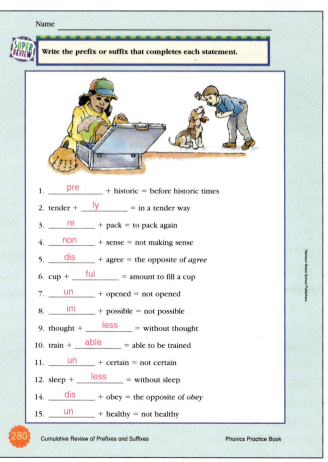

1. _pre_ + historic = before historic times
2. tender + _ly_ = in a tender way
3. _re_ + pack = to pack again
4. _non_ + sense = not making sense
5. _dis_ + agree = the opposite of *agree*
6. cup + _ful_ = amount to fill a cup
7. _un_ + opened = not opened
8. _im_ + possible = not possible
9. thought + _less_ = without thought
10. train + _able_ = able to be trained
11. _un_ + certain = not certain
12. sleep + _less_ = without sleep
14. _dis_ + obey = the opposite of *obey*
15. _un_ + healthy = not healthy

Cumulative Review of Prefixes and Suffixes — Phonics Practice Book

Page 281

Name _____

Add *-er* and *-est* to each word. Write the new words in the chart.

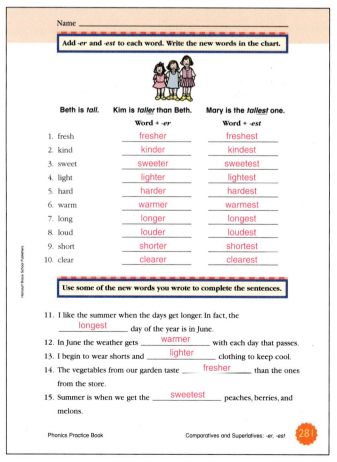

Beth is *tall*.   Kim is *taller* than Beth.   Mary is the *tallest* one.

	Word + -er	Word + -est
1. fresh	fresher	freshest
2. kind	kinder	kindest
3. sweet	sweeter	sweetest
4. light	lighter	lightest
5. hard	harder	hardest
6. warm	warmer	warmest
7. long	longer	longest
8. loud	louder	loudest
9. short	shorter	shortest
10. clear	clearer	clearest

Use some of the new words you wrote to complete the sentences.

11. I like the summer when the days get longer. In fact, the _longest_ day of the year is in June.
12. In June the weather gets _warmer_ with each day that passes.
13. I begin to wear shorts and _lighter_ clothing to keep cool.
14. The vegetables from our garden taste _fresher_ than the ones from the store.
15. Summer is when we get the _sweetest_ peaches, berries, and melons.

Phonics Practice Book — Comparatives and Superlatives: -er, -est

Phonics Practice Book Teacher's Edition 73

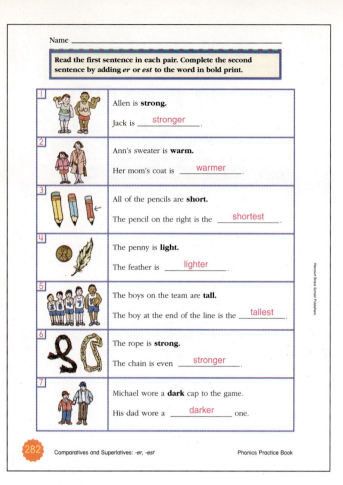
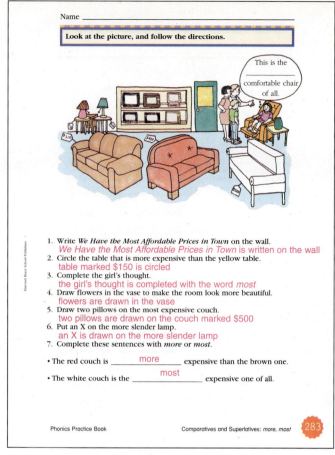
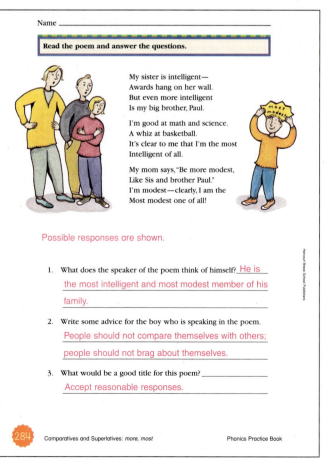
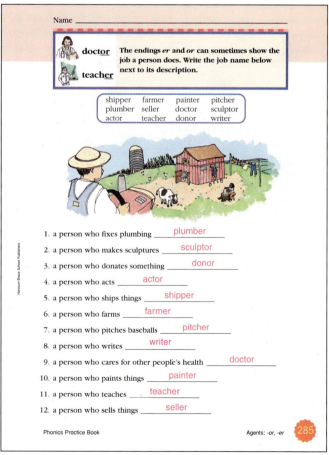

Name _____

Write the word that best completes each sentence.

> writer actor farmer
> painter sculptor plumber
> doctor officer speaker teacher

It's fun to think about the jobs I could have someday. I like to put things together. Once I saw a ___plumber___ putting the pipes and drains in a new house. I also like to make old things look new. I once saw a ___painter___ make an old house look great by putting fresh paint on it.

I like music and the arts, too. I love to put my hands in clay and make things from it, so I might become a ___sculptor___. I enjoy thinking up new stories and writing them on paper. It might be fun to be a ___writer___, and have people read my stories. I like to act stories out, too. I wonder if I could be a movie or television ___actor___.

Since I am good at growing things, I might become a ___farmer___. I like to help other people learn new things, so I might make a good ___teacher___. It would be exciting to be a police ___officer___ to help people stay safe. Or maybe I will become a ___doctor___ and help people stay healthy.

Since I have so many ideas about jobs, maybe I'll spend more time speaking with others about their jobs. That's it—I'll become a famous ___speaker___!

286 Agents: -or, -er

Name _____

Write the words that will make each sentence tell about the picture. REVIEW

> younger   fastest   smartest
> livelier   most beautiful
> more upset   more colorful

1		The girl on the left is ___younger___ than the girl on the right.
2		I think Mr. Martinez is the ___smartest___ teacher in the school.
3		The baby that is crying is ___more upset___ than the other one.
4		The painting that Joanne is holding is ___more colorful___ than the other painting.
5		This man is the ___fastest___ shipper at the factory.
6		Rosa is picking the ___most beautiful___ flowers to give to her grandmother.
7		The puppy on the left is ___livelier___ than the one on the right.

Review of Comparatives and Superlatives: -er, -est, more, most. Agents: -or, -er   287

Name _____

REVIEW Read the story, and answer the questions.

The people in my family have the most interesting jobs. My mom is a (doctor). She sees all kinds of patients. Some are older than she is. She also sees the youngest people in town—the babies. The people here tell us she is the most trusted (doctor) in town.

My dad is a famous (sculptor). He gives art shows in our town and in the city. The shows in the city are bigger. My dad likes to speak with the people who come to look at his work. He is one of the liveliest (speakers) around. The people in our town go to his shows both here and in the city. They say my dad makes them feel famous, too, because he lives in their town.

I wonder what job I will have when I grow up. I might be a house (painter) like my Aunt. Or, I could be a symphony (conductor) like Grandpa. Maybe my choice will be clearer to me when I get to middle school!

Possible responses are shown.

1. What would be a good title for this story?
   Different Kinds of Jobs

2. What do the people in the town say about their doctor?
   She is the most trusted doctor in town.

3. What does the storyteller say about deciding what job to have?
   Maybe the choice will be clearer in middle school.

Now underline the words in the story that compare. Circle the words that tell what kind of job a person has.

288 Review of Comparatives and Superlatives: -er, -est, more, most; Agents: -or, -er

---

Name _____

Write the word from the box that completes each sentence. SUPER REVIEW

> slowly   sugarless   farmer   impossible
> editor   nonsense   painter   portable
> most   cheerful

1. The turtle moved along ___slowly___.
2. Sheri always has a smile and a ___cheerful___ word for everyone.
3. We watched the ___painter___ mix the colors and get the brushes ready.
4. The ___editor___ checked the writer's spelling.
5. I like silly cartoons, comic strips, and other ___nonsense___.
6. My dentist says to try to eat ___sugarless___ snacks for healthy teeth.
7. My mom says that few things are ___impossible___ if you try your hardest.
8. We have a ___portable___ crib for my baby sister to use when we go places.
9. That surprise party was the ___most___ thoughtful thing anyone has ever done for me.
10. Todd's uncle is a ___farmer___ in Texas.

Cumulative Review of Prefixes, Suffixes, Comparatives and Superlatives, and Agents   289

Phonics Practice Book Teacher's Edition   75

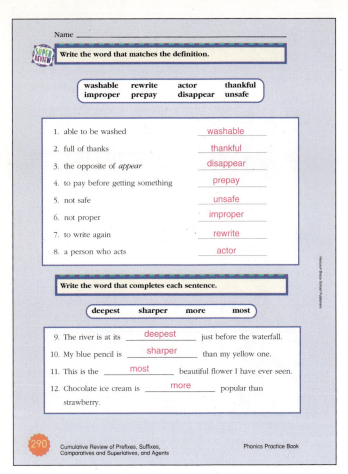
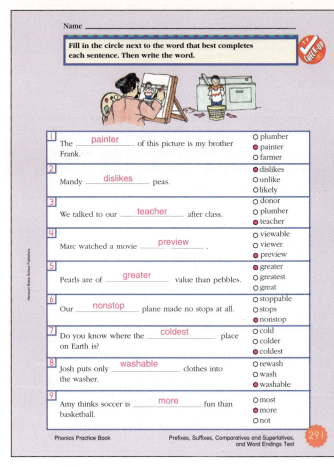
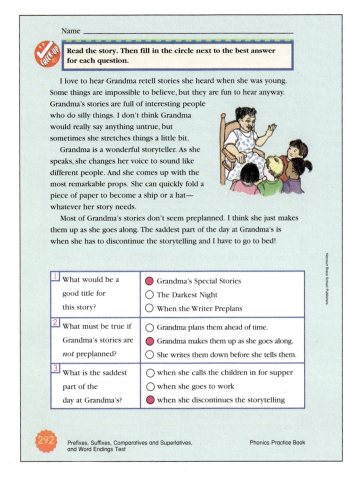
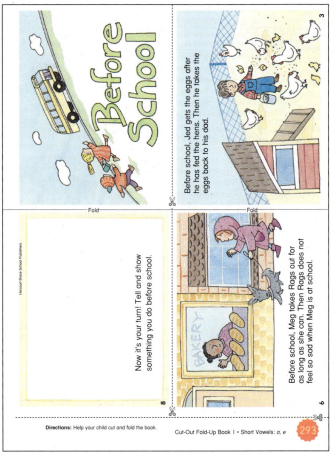

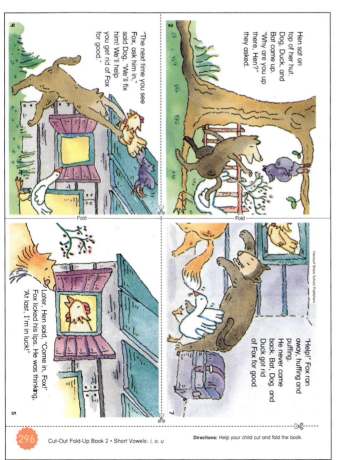

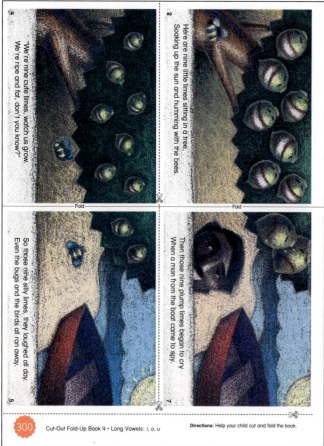
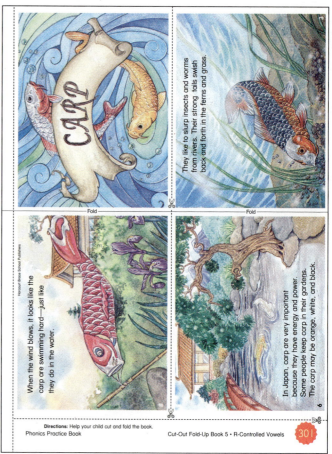

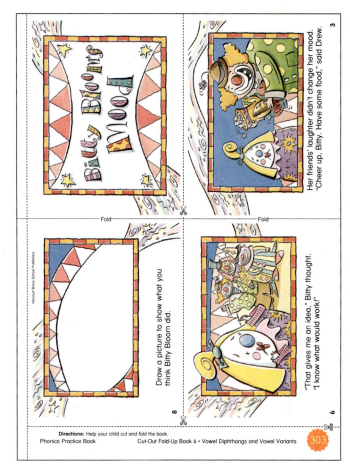

Phonics Practice Book Teacher's Edition

79